Problem Regions of Europe
General Editor **D. I. Scargill**

The Franco-Belgian Border Region
Hugh Clout

Oxford University Press 1975

Oxford University Press, Ely House, London W.1

Glasgow New York Toronto Melbourne Wellington
Cape Town Ibadan Nairobi Dar es Salaam Lusaka Addis Ababa
Delhi Bombay Calcutta Madras Karachi Lahore Dacca
Kuala Lumpur Singapore Hong Kong Tokyo

The author wishes to thank Margaret Thomas of the
Cartographic Unit at University College London,
for preparing the maps and diagrams, and the staffs
of the Mission Régionale (Lille), the Association pour
l'Expansion Industrielle de la Région Nord/Pas-de-
Calais, and the Ministère des Affaires Economiques
(Brussels) for supplying information.

Filmset by BAS Printers Limited, Wallop, Hampshire
and printed in Great Britain
at the University Press, Oxford
by Vivian Ridler, Printer to the University

Editor's Preface

Great economic and social changes have taken place in Europe in recent years. The agricultural workforce in the west was halved, for example, during the 1950s and 1960s. This unprecedented flight from the land has made possible some much-needed reorganization of farm holdings but it has also created problems, not least that of finding uses for land in the highlands and elsewhere where it is no longer profitable to farm. Closely related is the difficulty of maintaining services to a much diminished rural population or of providing new kinds of services for the holidaymakers who increasingly buy up rural properties.

Contraction of the labour force has also taken place in many traditional industries. The coal-mining industry alone has shed two-thirds of its workforce since 1950. The resulting problems have been especially serious in those mining or manufacturing districts which have a high level of dependence on a single source of employment—a not uncommon result of Europe's industrial past—and the efforts of those who seek to attract new industries are often thwarted by a legacy of pollution, bad housing, and soured labour relations.

Quite a different set of problems has arisen in the great cities of Europe such as London and Paris and in the conurbations of closely linked cities well exemplified by Randstad Holland. Here are problems due to growth brought about by the expansion of consumer-orientated manufacturing and still more by the massive increase in office jobs which proliferate in 'down-town' business districts. The problems are economic, social and political, and they include the effects of congestion, of soaring land values, of the increasing divorce of place of residence from place of work, and of the difficulty of planning a metropolitan region that may be shared between many independent-minded local authorities.

The problems resulting from change are not passing ones; indeed they exhibit a persistence that amply justifies their study on an areal basis. Hence the *Problem Regions of Europe* series. The volumes in the series have all been written by geographers who, by the nature of their discipline, can take a broadly based approach to description and analysis. Geographers in the past have been reluctant to base their studies on problem regions since the problem was often of a temporary nature, less enduring than the 'personality' of the region but the magnitude of present-day problems has even resulted in the suggestion that regions should be defined in terms of the problems that confront them.

Certain themes emerge clearly when the basis of the problem is examined: the effects of a harsh environment, of remoteness and of political division, as well as of industrial decay or urban congestion. But these have not been examined in isolation and the studies that make up the series have been carefully chosen in order that useful comparisons can be made. Thus, for example, both the Mezzogiorno and Andalusia have to contend with the problems of Mediterranean drought, wind, and flood, but the precise nature of these and other problems, as well as man's response to them, differs in the two regions. Similarly, the response to economic change is not the same in North-East England as in North Rhine–Westphalia, nor the response to social pressures the same in Paris as in the Randstad.

The efforts which individual governments have made to grapple with their problems provides a basis for critical assessment in each of the volumes. For too long, solutions were sought that were piecemeal and short-term. Our own Development Areas in Britain provide a good illustration of this kind of policy. Of late, however, European governments have shown an increasing awareness of the need to undertake planning on a regional basis. The success or otherwise of such regional policies is fully explored in the individual *Problem Region* volumes.

When it was first planned the *Problem Region* series was thought of as useful only to the sixth-form student of geography. As it has developed it has become clear that the authors— all specialists in the geography of the areas concerned—have contributed studies that will be useful, not only for sixth-form work, but as a basis for the more detailed investigations undertaken by advanced students, both of geography and of European studies in general.

D.I.S.

St. Edmund Hall, Oxford

Contents

1 The Region and its Problems

An international problem region

In several parts of modern Europe common economic and social problems are found on either side of an international frontier. As a result, 'international problem regions' may be recognized, each comprising parts of two or more countries. The problem region under examination in this book is of that type, covering the northernmost section of France and neighbouring areas in Belgium. It has a long history of urban development, coal-mining, and various types of industrial production, but in the present century traditional forms of employment have declined and large numbers of replacement jobs have been needed. Old urban environments and systems of communication have become out-dated and require renovation or replacement for use in the future.

These are the key problems and planning challenges that characterize the problem region bisected by the Franco-Belgian border. Unfortunately, there is no convenient title for this stretch of country which does not correspond exactly to administrative units or to 'natural regions' recognized by reference to drainage, geology, or other facts of physical geography. However, the French *départements* of the Nord and the Pas-de-Calais, together forming the planning region of the Nord, may be taken to represent one distinct part of the border zone. In Belgium our discussion will range more widely, to incorporate not only the textile-producing areas of the Flemish provinces but also the coal basins and industrial areas of Wallonia from the French frontier to Liège. Only brief mention will be made of the axis of economic growth extending from the Dutch Randstad through Antwerp and sections of Belgian Flanders to Brussels. The major planning problems of this latter stretch of territory are concerned with accommodating recent demographic and industrial expansion, rather than attempting to correct deficiencies inherited from earlier periods of economic greatness.

In the past, intensive agriculture, craft industries, and flourishing trade combined to support high densities of population in towns and villages on both sides of what is now the boundary between France and Belgium. In the eighteenth and nineteenth centuries the region's traditional range of employment was enlarged as mechanized industrial production, using coal from local pits, was added to old-established textile manufacture and other craft activities, which were themselves modified and mechanized. Urban growth continued apace as old trading cities expanded, small villages 'mushroomed' into manufacturing towns, and successive new mining settlements were built in the coal basins that extend for 300 km from the Pas-de-Calais through Wallonia to Aachen. The early phases of Europe's 'industrial revolution' were acted out in the coal-producing areas of what is now southern Belgium. But they had been preceded by a couple of centuries by the beginnings of the 'agricultural revolution', which had occurred farther to the west in Flanders. Between 1850 and 1914 the economic supremacy of the coalfields was unchallenged by major technological innovations in other industries, and also avoided serious disruption in war, but World War I ended that period of unrivalled growth as the appearance of new forms of energy brought advantages to areas beyond the coalfields.

By contrast with past splendour, the economic prestige of the Franco-Belgian Border Region has experienced serious setbacks since 1900 as its traditional sources of employment have failed to withstand powerful competition. The coal industry adjusted painfully to competition from cheaper energy sources in the form of imported oil, natural gas, and coking coal from the U.S.A. Textile producers lost markets as overseas countries developed their own cloth industries, based on lower labour costs, and as European consumers became increasingly concerned with new fabrics, rather than traditional cotton, linen, and woollen cloths. In a similar way, steel and metallurgical industries on coalfield sites faced competition from new plant in coastal areas, better placed for importing fuel and ores and for exporting finished products.

Attracting replacement jobs, renovating the built environment, and modernizing the communications network, have emerged as the common planning objectives of this international problem region. But, of course, economic development on either side of the national boundary has been geared to the particular

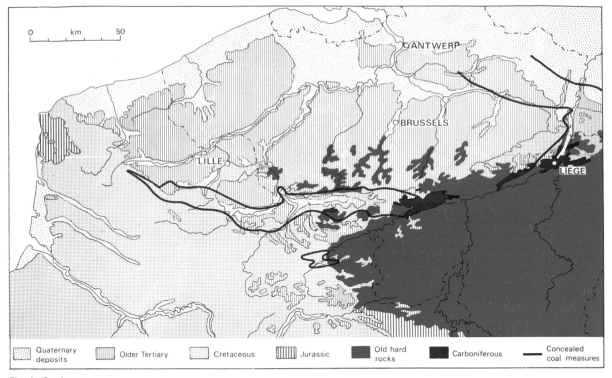

Fig. 1. Geology

Legend: Quaternary deposits | Older Tertiary | Cretaceous | Jurassic | Old hard rocks | Carboniferous | Concealed coal measures

conditions and demands of each of the countries concerned. The position of the northern frontier of France has changed many times over past centuries and Belgian independence was achieved only in the 1830s. Within Belgium there is the critical cultural divide between Flemish-speakers and French-speakers, which cuts across the problem region that has been defined. This cultural divide is very ancient but nonetheless is the root cause of many controversial issues in the economic, political, and social life of modern Belgium.

The region as a zone of transition

The Franco-Belgian problem region is distinctive in several respects, sometimes displaying features of a zone of transition, but also containing sharp lines of contrast. The idea of transition is appropriate to some aspects of both physical and human geography. The problem region represents an area of transition between the physical provinces of the Paris Basin to the south and the Rhine deltalands to the northeast. But it also contains a great variety of geological formations arranged east to west and ranging from the old, hard rocks of the Ardennes through the geological succession to the clays and other recent deposits of the Flanders Plain

(Fig. 1). The national boundary runs transversely across these geographical units and thus incorporates sections of each in both countries.

The drainage pattern is asymmetrical with main rivers, such as the Lys, Schelde, Sambre, and Meuse, running northwards through France and Belgium to reach the North Sea via the estuaries of the Schelde or the Dutch Maas (Fig. 2). However the natural pattern of waterways has been modified by centuries of canal-building, thereby improving navigation along existing watercourses, providing cross-country water links between Belgian rivers, and giving northern France access to her own Channel ports and to the focus of French economic and political power in the heart of the Paris Basin. The significance of the international frontier is illustrated by the fact that canals and rivers crossing it have been managed in different ways on the two sides to accommodate vessels of differing sizes. French canals have normally been left shallower than those in Belgium, thereby preventing invasion of the trading hinterland of the port of Dunkirk by goods carried in large barges from Antwerp or Rotterdam.

The great mineral-rich contact zone linking the North European Plain with upland areas further south extends in an east-west direction from Russia to France and cuts across the Franco-Belgian problem region, endowing it with deposits of iron-ore and coal. The contact zone has long functioned as an axis of movement and trade, with natural routeways through the Meuse and Sambre valleys to the east, and the Schelde and Lys to the west, converging in northern France before leading southward into the core of the Paris Basin. In addition, the region commands land access to the narrowest crossing points on the English Channel, with important ports being established on the coasts of northern France and Belgium. The Channel itself is the busiest axis of world trade, located at a tangent to the western edge of the region.

In terms of population density, the Franco-Belgian Border Region represents a transition from the relatively empty northern parts of the Paris Basin to the densely-peopled Rhinelands (Fig. 3). Very high densities are found along the coalfield axis, which experienced the peak of its economic prosperity during the nineteenth century, and along the Flanders axis, where towns and cities from Artois to Ghent flourished as centres of cloth-making and trade from much earlier times. The population density of 308 persons per km² in the Nord region is three times the French national average (91 per km²) and half as high again as the average for Wallonia (180 per km²), which contains the rural Ardennes

as well as major industrial areas, lagging behind Belgian Flanders (375 per km²) and the small bilingual Brussels region (1300 per km²).

Lines of contrast

Distinct from these transitional aspects of physical and human geography, two dividing-lines cut abruptly through the problem region. One of these is cultural and the other, political. The cultural and linguistic divide in Belgium between Dutch-speakers (Flemings) and French-speakers (Walloons) derives from the Frankish invasions of the fourth and fifth centuries A.D. (Fig. 8). The Franks settling north of the divide used a Germanic language but inhabitants further south used Latin forms of speech that were later to develop into French. Sparsely-populated woodland across the centre of what is now Belgium acted as a buffer between the two groups. The dividing-line originally extended as far south as Artois but it retreated gradually under pressure from French speakers. However, the language divide cutting east-west through Belgium has remained virtually unchanged since medieval times.

By contrast with this ancient cultural division, the boundary between France and Belgium is of recent origin. The problem region has been fought over many times through the centuries in wars varying in scale from local scuffles to the

Fig. 2. Drainage and Relief

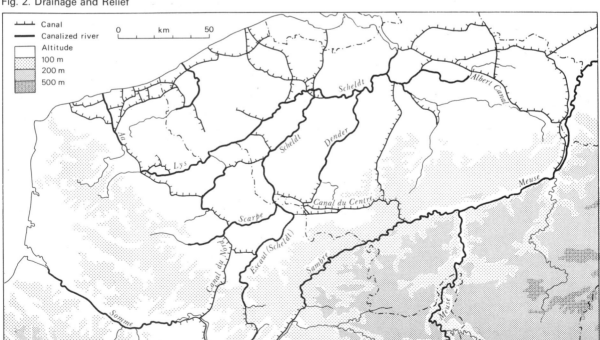

7

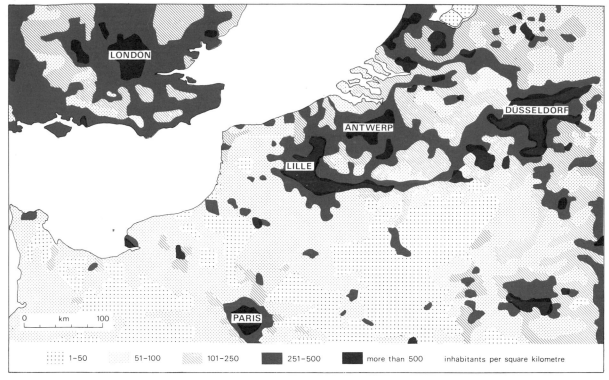

Fig. 3. Population Densities: the Franco-Belgian Border Region in its West European Setting (*Oréam-Nord*, p. 22)

Fig. 4. Acquisition of Territory by France Along its Northern Frontier (Source: *Oréam-Nord: Aménagement d'une Région Urbaine: Le Nord/Pas-de-Calais,* République Française, Circonscription d'Action Régionale Nord, p. 17)

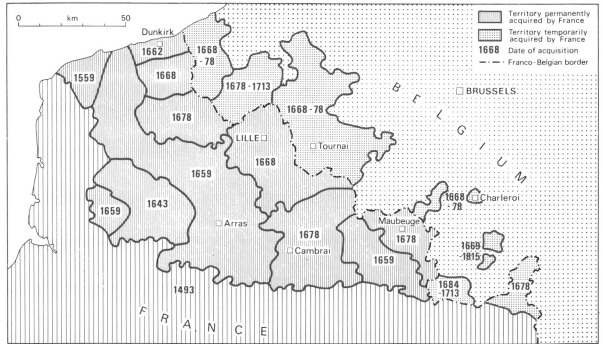

two world wars. In Professor Pierre George's words '. . . it was on the plains of Flanders, in the forests and marshes of the east, that the decisive battles were fought . . . the outcome of wars was decided on the Yser, the Sambre, the Meuse, and between the Vosges and the Ardennes' (1973, pp. 5–6). The State of France gradually acquired fragments of territory and expanded northwards from its focus in the heart of the Paris Basin (Fig. 4). The resultant international boundary is totally arbitrary in alignment and between the North Sea and the Ardennes follows a 'natural' division for only 25 km along the river Lys.

In 1648 the Dutch acquired their independence but the southern part of the Low Countries (modern Belgium) remained under Spanish rule, to pass into Austrian hands in 1713. Following the French Revolution of 1789, French invaders controlled the whole of the Low Countries from Paris as part of their Empire between 1794 and 1814. Then the balance of power changed and both halves of the Low Countries were joined under the King of Holland, William of Orange, to form the reunited Kingdom of the Netherlands, which was recognized by the Treaty of Vienna (1815). This association was short-lived, with serious administrative blunders taking place. In 1830 the population of the South, predominantly Catholic and French-speaking, rose in a rebellion which led to the creation of a separate Belgian state the actual boundaries of which were determined by the great powers, Britain and France. Flemings and Walloons in this way became members of a single nation, but the ruling class was French-speaking and French was the official language. Flemings sought linguistic recognition after 1860 but Belgium did not become bilingual officially until 1898. In the nineteenth century the Walloon South was the more urbanized, industrialized, and economically progressive part of the country. Rural Flanders was relatively underdeveloped, but Flemish solidarity developed against the cultural and numerical dominance of French speakers.

All this has changed in the present century, as the old-established industrial economy of southern Belgium has contracted and the Flemish population and economy has grown rapidly. The political implications of these changes have been very important, with Flemings tending to be more conservative and Roman Catholic in outlook than Walloons, who have greater socialist and trades-union sympathies. In 1932 a language law re-emphasized the significance of the linguistic division between the two groups. North of the linguistic divide Flemish was decreed to be the sole language for administration and education. To the south French was to be used exclusively, with Brussels being a bilingual area where both languages had equal status. The language issue still affects all aspects of daily life in Belgium. It is normal for Walloons and Flemings to live in their own parts of the country without making much contact. They attend linguistically-appropriate schools and colleges, marry within their own language group, and choose their shops and other daily activities on the criterion of language. The kingdom of the Belgians has not proved to be a cultural 'melting pot'. As the proportion of Walloons in the national population declines, French-speaking Belgians fear domination by Flemish interests and the introduction of pro-Flemish policies to the detriment of the South.

Textiles and metalworking

To appreciate the causes of the modern economic and social problems of the Franco-Belgian problem region, it is necessary to examine earlier phases of development and trace how the region's urban and industrial inheritance came into being. In the Middle Ages many features of the traditional industrial economy of Flanders and surrounding areas were already in evidence. By the mid-twelfth century powerful urban communities had developed important cloth-making functions using yarn that had been spun in the countryside by farmers and their families who worked at spinning during slack periods of the agricultural year. Towns in the area bounded by Bruges, Ghent, Cambrai and Saint-Omer had earned Europe-wide reputations for the excellence of their woollen cloths, produced from the fleeces of Flemish sheep, and of their linen made from local flax retted in the lime-free water of the river Lys.

To the south, iron-making and metal-refining were well established in Wallonia. Iron-smelting was focused on the northern slopes of the Ardennes upland, using local haematite ore, charcoal from local beechwoods and other sources of timber, and abundant supplies of flowing water. In the valleys of the Sambre and the Meuse, towns such as Dinant, Huy, Liège, and Namur produced iron castings, nails, locks, edged tools, and armaments and also goods manufactured from brass and copper. At this early stage coal was already being mined in small quantities from shallow workings in the folded and faulted basins where coal measures outcropped along the Meuse valley, between Liège and Namur, and along the Sambre valley towards Charleroi. To the west of the latter town, coal measures were concealed beneath more recent deposits and the development of that part of the coalfield had to wait until the eighteenth and nineteenth centuries when techniques for deep mining were improved. Coal was employed in increasing quantities in the flourishing craft industries of Wallonia.

As early as the thirteenth century iron-making had become a settled and permanent activity in the region, whereas in other parts of Europe it still involved the transportation of moveable forges to exploit small local reserves of iron-ore and timber for charcoal. Venetian glass-workers moved to sites near Charleroi during the fourteenth century and established another element in the diverse industrial economy of Wallonia. By the mid-sixteenth century iron forges around Namur were described as '. . . so innumerable that the whole country seemeth to be Vulcan's forge'. During that century the iron, glass, and chemical industries of Liège were particularly dynamic, with important manufacturing linkages being developed between individual crafts. Coal production flourished not only to supply local industries but also for dispatch along the Meuse to Holland and Zeeland, where it competed with coals from Newcastle upon Tyne, and along the Rhine as far south as Frankfurt-on-Main.

The leading textile-producing areas were in Flanders between Artois and Ghent, but one branch flourished in Wallonia. That was the woollen industry of the Vesdre valley, which processed fleeces from the Ardennes and from Upper Silesia. Labour was cheap and unhampered by the numerous restrictions that had been imposed by the gilds of Flanders. During the seventeenth century the Vesdre valley turned to producing fine-quality cloths, in place of the coarser woollens that had been manufactured in earlier times.

Agricultural advance

Flanders and Wallonia were important in respects other than manufacturing. Growing numbers of craft workers needed to be fed from local farmlands which became the hearth of the European 'agricultural revolution'. As early as the fifteenth century, farming in Flanders and the Low Countries had become intensified, allowing large quantities of food to be produced from very limited land resources. Fallowing of land was eliminated and fodder crops and legumes were grown instead. Soil fertility was ensured by applying heavy dressings of manure, from livestock fed on the fodder crops, and by using night-soil from Flemish towns and peat ashes brought by barge from the peatfields of the Netherlands. Low-lying areas were drained efficiently. The popular saying that the Flemings had 'manufactured' good soils from very indifferent physical resources was certainly true. New implements, such as the Brabant plough, were brought into use and new crops were grown. These included oil seeds, buckwheat, hops, madder, and many types of vegetable. By the mid-seventeenth century, the 'agricultural revolution' that was soon to affect Norfolk and other parts of England had already taken place in Brabant, Flanders, and the Low Countries. But, when compared with Flemish standards, agricultural conditions on the northernmost sections of the plateaux of the Paris Basin still remained primitive.

The rise of coal mining

During the seventeenth and eighteenth centuries coal-based manufacturing flourished in Wallonia and mining techniques improved, with steam engines being used to pump water from coal pits after 1720. The advantages of coal for fuelling industrial activities were revealed to the French who had occupied the Mons coal basin between 1701 and 1709. The French invested in that coalfield and industries in northern France became partially reliant upon Mons coal, but the Treaty of Utrecht (1713) transferred the coal basin to Austrian control, and as a result dues had to be paid on coal transported into France. The search for a westward extension of the coalfield into France continued with vigour. In 1716 very poor coal was discovered north of Valenciennes but not until 1734 were the bituminous deposits of Anzin found. At that time the coal industry of northern France was born. By 1789, 4000 miners were employed on the Anzin concession, which had an annual output of 300 000 tonnes. In addition, there were 340 miners on the Aniche concession extracting 4000 tonnes per annum. Sales of coal to Paris were restricted because of poor transport conditions, but these improved in the first quarter of the nineteenth century with the construction of the Saint Quentin canal.

English techniques of iron-making were established in Wallonia, linked with the name of the Lancashire family of Cockerill, whose members started making textile machinery at Verviers in 1797. John Cockerill turned to making iron at the Château de Seraing near Liège, where the first coke-fired blast furnace on the Continent was opened in 1827, with a second established almost immediately afterwards at Charleroi. Within ten years, one-third of the furnaces in the Liège region were coke-fired and local coal production rose from 330 000 tonnes in 1815 to 1·2 million tonnes in 1850. Wallonia was far in advance of other

industrial areas nearby. The first coke furnace in northern France was built in 1830 using Belgian coke but the second was not constructed until 1837. In the Ruhr the first coke furnaces came only after 1845. During the first half of the nineteenth century Verviers and surrounding towns were also the most progressive woollen-producing centres on the Continent. The Belgian uprising and subsequent independence threatened the Sambre-Meuse industrial areas with a loss of industrial sales in France. But the decision to build a Belgian railway network was taken as early as 1834 and the industries of Wallonia were linked to ports and major cities elsewhere in Belgium.

In 1840 the Anzin concession was producing over 70 per cent of the coal mined in northern France, where five large companies were responsible for 99 per cent of local output. At mid-century the coalfield in Nord *département*, with an annual output of 1 million tonnes, was still however the poor relation of the coalfields of Wallonia (6·25 million tonnes p.a.), and the Ruhr (1·70 million tonnes p.a.). But the start of mining after 1847 from the concealed extension of the Valenciennes coalfield which stretched westward into Pas-de-Calais *département* soon allowed all that to change (Fig. 5). Development of the concealed coalfield attracted vast amounts of capital between 1850 and 1875, with production from mines in the Pas-de-Calais outstripping that from the Nord. By the mid-1860s output from the joint Nord/Pas-de-Calais field was greater than that from the coalfields of central France. Five million tonnes were mined in northern France in 1872, and annual output was subsequently doubled by 1886. At the end of the century, 20 million tonnes were mined each year from over a hundred mines managed by three dozen operators in the northern French coalfield. Some 15 million tonnes of that total came from the Pas-de-Calais. The coalfield was controlled by a number of powerful entrepreneurial families, who had also acquired an important share in the railway companies of northern France.

Just as an iron and steel industry had developed in many parts of the Walloon coal basins so it was established in the eastern section of the coalfield of northern France. The first blast furnace using local coal was built at Denain in 1837 and by the 1850s the iron industry had become firmly established in that town and in Valenciennes. Another branch developed in the Sambre valley at Maubeuge and in the neighbouring Avesnois area, using raw materials

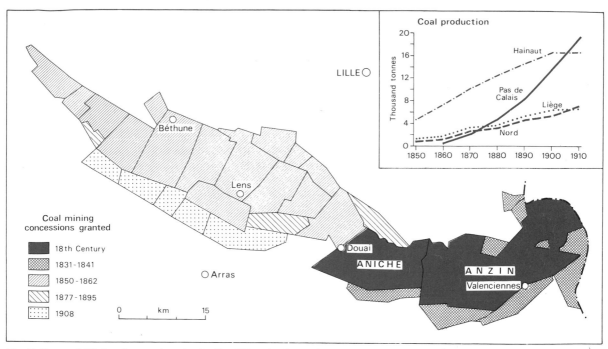

Fig. 5. Dates of Mining Concessions in the Nord/Pas-de-Calais Coalfield; and Graph of Coal Production in Northern France and Southern Belgium (1850–1910) (Sources: M. Gillet, *loc, cit.*, 1969, and statistics from E. A. Wrigley, *op. cit.*, 1961)

Fig. 6. Distribution of Urban Settlements

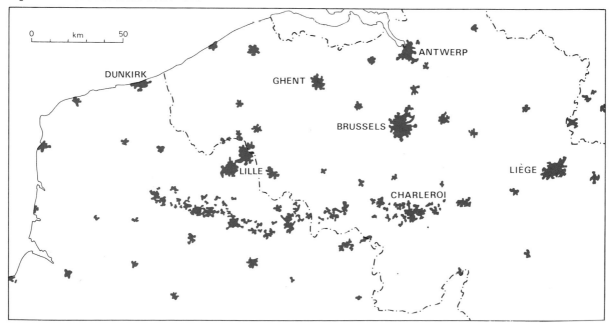

from Belgium to replace local supplies of ore and charcoal. By contrast, the concealed section of the coalfield to the west remained primarily concerned with mining. Northern France was still a small producer of iron goods by comparison with other sections of the coalfield industrial zone of north-western Europe (Table 1).

TABLE I
Production of pig iron in 1851 (tonnes)

Northern France	49 000	Liège	77 000
Ruhr	11 500	Hainaut	71 000
Aachen	11 000	Wallonia	148 000

Textile production became increasingly mechanized, with Lille, Roubaix, and Tourcoing rising as cloth capitals. It was in this industry that the fortunes of many of the bourgeois families of northern France were made. In contrast with earlier phases, spinning had now become an urban activity. Production of cotton cloths gained importance, as linen-making became less significant. Similar trends operated in eastern Flanders. English looms for cotton-weaving had been introduced to Ghent in 1798 and, from there, cotton manufacture spread into the Dendre and Schelde valleys. Application of steam power to the textile industry occurred in the mid-nineteenth century, for example in Lille, where there had been 130 steam engines in use in textile mills in 1848 but eighteen years later the figure had risen to 576.

Coal extraction, expansion of the iron and steel industry, and application of steam-powered mechanization to the old textile industry, were paralleled by large-scale urbanization and changes in communication networks. Settlements for miners, factory workers, and their families 'mushroomed' during the nineteenth century and the early years of the twentieth century, disrupting the regular pattern of towns and villages that had been in existence since medieval times (Fig. 6). The harshness of life in the mining settlements of northern France during the nineteenth century was captured by Emile Zola in his novel *Germinal*. Sometimes the new industrial settlements were equipped with adequate services but more often than not they grew without suitable provision being made.

Canals and railways

Communications were improved to ease the transportation of raw materials and the distribution of manufactured goods. Already by the early nineteenth century a dense road system had been complemented by shallow canals with dimensions suited to the size of vessels and volume of traffic handled at that time (Fig. 2). For example, coal mined at Anzin could reach all parts of northern France by canal in 1800, but river systems, roads, and early canals afforded access from northern France to the Channel coast and into Belgium rather more easily than to Paris. Links between the northern frontier province and the French capital were soon improved, however, when the Saint Quentin canal was constructed (1810–24) and key features of the railway network were built joining Paris to Lille, Valenciennes, and other major towns of northern France (1846–55). Additional lines were built later, with railways in the Pas-de-Calais coalfield taking over the role that canals had played in opening up the Nord section of the coalfield during the eighteenth century. Railway construction in Belgium came even earlier than in France. By 1842 the Government had constructed lines from Liège and Mons to Malines, thence to the Belgian ports and the textile towns of Flanders. The vital railway spine through industrial Wallonia was added later in the century.

At the beginning of the twentieth century northern France and neighbouring Belgian areas in Flanders and Wallonia displayed many of the features of nineteenth-century industrial strength, their towns supported by cloth-making, coal-mining, and the manufacture of iron, steel, and metallurgical goods. But changing economic circumstances were soon to turn this strength into a weakness that was to reach crisis proportions after 1945.

3   From Strength to Weakness

Economic stagnation

Relatively little was done to modernize the key economic activities of the Franco-Belgian problem region between the wars. In the words of Professor José Sporck of the University of Liège '. . . in 1947 the industrial areas of Wallonia contained an out-dated industrial structure, almost identical to that at the beginning of the century' (1970, p. 58). The same was true of northern France. In addition, old settlements and systems of communication were unsuited to post-war needs. Problems resulting from the rundown of coal extraction were to be particularly severe, since mining had become a way of life on the coalfields as well as a key economic activity for the whole problem region.

Decline of the coal industry

At the opening of the twentieth century the coalfield of northern France produced about 20 million tonnes of coal each year, some two-thirds of the French total output. The Walloon coal basins accounted for the entire Belgian output since, although the deep reserves of the Campine field had been discovered in 1901, they were not exploited until after 1917. In the following decades the coalfields of northern France and southern Belgium emerged as expensive areas to work. Seams were usually less than one metre thick and were sometimes less than half that amount. By 1938, average yields per manshift in northern France were only 1100 kg, by comparison with 1600 kg in the Saar, 2000 kg in the Ruhr, and 2400 kg in Dutch Limburg. Nevertheless, the output of 28 million tonnes of coal from northern France was substantially higher than it had been at the beginning of the century.

Immediately after World War II the coal industries of both parts of the Franco-Belgian problem region were essential components in the drive for economic recovery, with mining being stimulated to provide vital fuel supplies. In 1954 René Gendarme wrote in his analysis of the Nord region that the coalfield '. . . will be indispensable not only to the national economy but also to the economy of Western Europe' (p. 284). This was a period of increasing coal production but also of rationalization and mechanization. In France, nationalization of the northern coal industry had been agreed in December 1944 and was enacted in May 1946. The number of pits was reduced from 125 on the eve of World War II to 28 in 1968. In 1947 over 220 000 workers were employed by the Northern Coal Board (Houillères du Bassin du Nord/Pas-de-Calais) but by 1969 the total had been cut to 75 000 and subsequently fell to 62 570 in 1971. That figure will be halved again by

TABLE 2

Employment in the French coal industry, 1947–71

	1947	1971	Percentage change
Nord/Pas-de-Calais	222 000	62 570	−72
Lorraine	45 640	25 000	−45
Other coal basins	89 050	23 870	−73
French total	356 690	111 440	−69

TABLE 3

The industrial structure of southern Belgium, 1947

Borinage	coal-mining, coke, carbochemicals, shoes
Centre	coal-mining, steel, mechanical construction, glass, pottery
Charleroi	steel, mechanical and electrical construction, coal, glass, chemicals
Basse-Sambre	coal, chemicals, glass
Liège	steel, mechanical construction, armaments, coal, chemicals, glass
Verviers	woollen textiles, leather, construction of textile machinery

1975 and the regional plan for the Nord and the Pas-de-Calais estimated the number of miners to be perhaps 8500 in 1985. Even this latter figure has seemed uncertain since proposals have been announced for terminating coal-mining in northern France by the mid-1980s. However, the oil-supply crisis which arose in 1973 adds an important element of uncertainty to the future of the coal industry.

In the 1950s and early 1960s the western sections of the coalfield in the Pas-de-Calais were being worked out and this contributed to the shrinkage of the labour force. Coal-mining in northern France and in the small coal basins of the Massif Central has been an expensive operation when compared with modernized mining in Lorraine, or with the purchase of imported oil, American coking coal, or Dutch natural gas. In the 1950s the coal industry of northern France released 2–2500 miners each year, but after the mid 1960s the number increased to 7000 and is now running at 10 000. (Table 2). Contraction and eventual termination of mining in the western section of the coalfield released thousands of workers onto the region's already weak employment market. Six thousand miners and their families moved house from the western section of the French coalfield to eastern areas, where production will continue for another decade at least.

In spite of these changes in employment, the volume of coal mined in northern France remained at about 29 million tonnes throughout the 1950s, falling slightly to 27 million tonnes in 1962. In 1968 plans were announced to halve national production from 50 million tonnes to 25 million tonnes in 1975, of which 10–11 million tonnes were to come from the northern coalfield. By 1971 the region was producing 15 million tonnes, ahead of Lorraine (11·5 million tonnes) and the Centre-Midi basins (8·5 million tonnes). Nevertheless, both the volume and the proportion of French coal mined in the North will probably decline rapidly in the future.

Very similar problems have been encountered in the coal basins and industrial areas of southern Belgium, stretching from the Borinage, through the Centre region, Charleroi, and the Lower Sambre valley, to Liège. However, the position of coal-mining in relation to other forms of employment varies considerably from basin to basin (Table 3). The coal crisis in Wallonia was latent in the 1930s but measures to deal with it were delayed during the years of post-war economic reconstruction. Attempts were made in the 1950s by the European Coal and Steel Community (E.C.S.C.) to prop up the industry by compensating for high production costs rather than modernizing installations. The loss of 260 lives in the Marcinelle mining disaster in August 1956 formed a tragic introduction to the coal crisis of southern Belgium. By 1958 the seriousness of the industry's problems was widely realized.

Rationalization schemes were put into operation in each of the south Belgian coal basins where coal seams averaged less than 70 cm in thickness and were seriously folded and faulted. Pits were closed and miners released. In the Borinage basin, for example, where the best coal was at depths of 880–1400 m, sixty pits had operated in 1900. By 1955 only twenty-three were worked, by seven companies, and five years later only three companies remained to operate ten pits.

In the mid-1960s the Belgian Government announced more stringent measures and thirty mines were closed in Wallonia between 1966 and 1969. Piping of natural gas from Groningen in the northern Netherlands hammered more nails into the coffin of the coal industry. Production throughout southern Belgium was cut back by 87 per cent, from 20·5 million tonnes in 1955, to 6·3 million tonnes in 1968, and 2·6 million tonnes in 1973 (Fig. 7). Output was also reduced from the Campine coalfield of north-eastern Belgium to lower national coal output by 70 per cent from 30·0 million tonnes in 1955 to 8·8 million tonnes in 1973. The bulk of E.C.S.C. financial aid to the Belgian coal industry during the 1960s was paid to Wallonia

Fig. 7. Coal Production in Belgium 1963–72, by coalfield

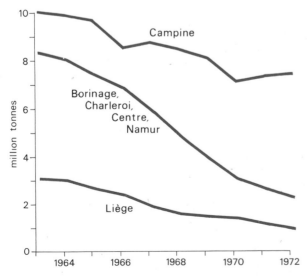

(1·2 billion Belgian francs) for reorganization, industrial retraining, and for assisting miners to move to areas where jobs were available. By contrast, only 300 million Belgian francs were awarded to the Campine. The net result has been to reduce the number of south-Belgian coal workers from almost 100 000 in 1955 to 20 700 in 1968 and 8800 in 1973 (6100 underground and 2700 surface workers).

Although serious in each of the coal basins, the decline was most intense in areas such as the Borinage and Centre which were largely geared to mining and lacked other buoyant staple industries. In the five years between 1958 and 1962 these two areas lost 36 000 jobs because of mine closures (31 000) and the release of labour from old-established metallurgical jobs and the building industry (5000). Only 2900 replacement jobs were created locally over the same period. However, not all the 36 000 jobs lost provoked unemployment. Some 11 000 miners close to retirement age were pensioned off. Others, including immigrant workers, were informed of alternative jobs still available in the mining areas of northern France and Federal Germany or elsewhere in southern Belgium, Brussels, and Flanders. The economies of the Charleroi and Liège basins were rather more broad-based than those of the Borinage and Centre and managed to absorb redundant miners more easily. Under E.C.S.C. plans, coal production in southern Belgium is scheduled to be terminated in the near future but, as in northern France, the energy crisis may modify that decision.

Rationalization of textile production

At the same time as the coal industry declined, other key industries also released workers. The textile industry of northern France and neighbouring Belgium involves an elliptical zone extending from Ghent to Arras and from Calais to Fourmies. It employs about 275 000 workers and helps support around one million people. Weaknesses in the woollen industry of Fourmies were apparent as early as the mid-nineteenth century, and the textile industry in all parts of the problem region experienced contraction in the depression years of the 1930s. In response to this condition, the last twenty-five years have witnessed important organizational changes in the textile industry. In the words of one French mill-owner '... 1950 was "prehistory" in the textile industry'. Now this activity is vitally concerned with moderniza-

tion and capital investment to replace labour with machines.

In the half-century before World War I there had been few technical changes in the industry, but electrification, use of automatic machinery, and better work organization brought changes in the 1920s and 1930s. Nevertheless, equipment remained quite simple and did not require highly-trained personnel. After 1945 factory owners visited the United States to learn American production techniques. At this time many traditional markets for basic types of textiles were lost as ex-colonial countries became industrialized, and cheap cloths were manufactured in India, Pakistan, and other Asian countries. In addition, tastes and fashions were altering in Western Europe and the domestic textile industry struggled to keep up with them. Many firms merged and more automatic machinery was brought into use.

The result of these changes has been to reduce the number of textile-workers in northern France from 224 000 before World War II, to 170 000 in 1954, and 121 000 in 1968 (Table 4). Estimates for 1985 are in the order of 95 500. In the past the region concentrated on woollens (employing 43 per cent of its textile workforce), cotton (29 per cent), and linen and canvas (21 per cent). Synthetic fibres and textile finishing work were poorly represented. Ninety per cent of the region's woollen-workers were concentrated in Roubaix and Tourcoing in the early 1960s, and an equal proportion of cotton-workers was employed in the latter towns, in Armentières, and in Lille. Redundancies among lace-workers in Calais and woollen-workers in Fourmies and Avesnes qualified those towns to be among the first 'development areas' designated in France for financial assistance in 1955 and 1958. However some branches of the textile industry have managed to increase their labour force in the past two decades. Thus the number of hosiery-workers rose from 9100 in 1954 to 16 500 in 1970, with increases taking place in towns such as Arras and Cambrai where large numbers of women workers are available. By contrast, employment in the hosiery industry of Roubaix and Tourcoing has stagnated.

Comparable trends have occurred in Belgian Flanders, with contraction affecting old-established sectors of the textile industry, such as flax-processing and linen-making in Courtrai and other West Flemish towns. Advances have been made in spinning and weaving of cotton, and production of high-quality textiles and synthetic fibres. But each of these branches is highly

TABLE 4
Changes in employment in the Nord Region, 1954–85*

	1954	1962	1968	1985 (median estimate)
Agriculture	166 641	128 822	104 380	73 500
All industry	727 505	709 396	681 500	690 000
Transport	56 331	55 312	52 420	67 000
Services	387 177	427 307	498 460	659 500
Total employed	1 337 654	1 320 837	1 336 760	1 490 000
Selected industrial branches				
Coal	143 609	112 123	87 380	8500
Steel	30 186	37 620	35 640	33 000
Non-ferrous metals	3 799	3 605	3 700	3 050
Cars and cycles	1 895	5 827	4 540	37 500
Textiles	169 998	140 049	121 000	95 500
Clothing	34 018	35 673	37 440	39 250

* Excluding workers commuting from Belgium each day

mechanized and requires a relatively small number of workers. Jobs have been lost from traditional sectors of the cotton industry in Ghent. Similarly the number of employees in the woollen mills of Verviers declined by 5000 during the 1960s. Whilst containing some dynamic features, the textile industry of northern France and neighbouring parts of Belgium is no longer the buoyant key element in the regional economy that it was in the past.

Partly because of the contraction of certain branches of the French textile industry, but also because of the introduction of new light industries in Belgian Flanders, the number of Belgians migrating daily to work in the textile mills and other factories of Roubaix, Tourcoing, and Lille has declined. The growth of each of these towns during the nineteenth century was partly due to the permanent immigration of Flemings from the overpopulated countryside of north-western Belgium. But costs of living and housing in Belgium were cheaper than in northern France and thus many Belgians preferred to commute into France on a daily basis from such border towns as Menin and Mouscron and from deeper in Belgian territory. The volume of daily cross-frontier commuters (*frontaliers*) has declined considerably, however, since the depression years of the 1930s. In contrast with earlier times, wage rates for comparable jobs are now higher in Belgium than in northern France. In the last decade alone, numbers entering Lille *arrondissement* from Belgium each day fell from 27 000 (in-cluding 19 500 male workers) to 16 000 (of whom 11 000 were men).

Changes in metallurgical production

Other traditional industries, such as steel manufacture and metallurgy, have experienced changes in employment and output since 1945. Three main metallurgical areas may be identified in northern France. Valenciennes, Denain, and nearby towns in the Schelde valley contain blast furnaces, rolling mills, and steelworks. Similar components are found in a second metallurgical area around Maubeuge in the Sambre valley. These works are supplied with local coking coal, with iron-ore brought by rail from Lorraine, and with local steel scrap. Coking coal is back-hauled by electrified railway from Valenciennes to the steel-making area of Thionville in Lorraine. As in other parts of Western Europe these long-established sectors of the industry have reduced their labour force in recent years. However, the number of workers in the steel industry of northern France declined by only 2000 between 1962 and 1968 (Table 4). This was because the third metallurgical area, at Dunkirk, experienced important increases in employment and production. Work on the Usinor coastal steelworks started in 1958 on a site reclaimed from the sea and in immediate proximity to special dock facilities for handling coking coal from the United States and high-quality iron-ore from Sweden and North Africa. In 1965 Usinor merged with the Lorraine-Escaut steel corporation, and the Dunkirk

17

works became the key feature in the corporation's plans for the future. By 1970, 4 million tonnes of steel were being produced at the Dunkirk plant, which employed 5800 workers. Proposals for expansion in the future have been announced. These will be discussed later.

Trends similar to those in the French Sambre and Schelde valleys took place in the steel-producing areas of Wallonia, using coking coal from local pits, the Campine and the Ruhr, and iron-ore from Lorraine and Sweden. Steelworks are found upstream of Liège, especially on the right bank of the river Meuse, and in the Centre and Charleroi areas. A new steelworks was opened in the 1960s downstream from Liège, between Herstal and the Dutch border. The metallurgical region of Liège also produces special steels for use in the electronics industry, locomotive construction, and in the manufacture of marine engines for the shipyards of Antwerp. Workshop firms produce armaments, castings, stampings, machine tools, and parts for cycles and motorcycles. Zinc production was pioneered by a Liègeois as early as 1798 and remains a distinctive element in the local metallurgical industry. Until the end of the nineteenth century local ores were used, but zinc concentrates are now imported from Australia, Peru, Sweden, and Zaïre. As in northern France, most of the traditional branches of Walloon metallurgy have been shedding labour in recent years. Yet, in Belgium as in France, a major new 'coastal' steelworks has been constructed, at Zelzate on a site alongside the deep-water canal 20 km from the western Schelde and 15 km north of Ghent. The works are fed by iron-ores from Sweden and North-West Africa, and coke from the Ruhr and Wallonia. Rolling mills and blast furnaces started operation in the mid-1960s. But this and most other innovations in Belgium's metallurgical industry have been located in the Flemish North rather than in Wallonia.

Housing problems

In addition to problems of declining employment in many old-established industries, the Franco-Belgian problem region has inherited out-dated patterns of settlement and communications. Three types of housing deficiency may be identified. The first involves the need to improve accommodation in rural parts of the region which require better provision of piped water, electricity, and mains drainage. The others are essentially urban problems. Wartime destruction in 1914–18 and 1939–45 necessitated reconstruction of many urban areas in northern France and Belgium, but two main housing problems nevertheless remain.

The first arises in those areas of industrial housing that were constructed rapidly in the textile towns of Flanders just before the middle years of the nineteenth century. Small industrial cottages built around courtyards (courées) in Lille, Roubaix, and Tourcoing typify this problem. Lille had a tradition of producing fine-quality cloths both in the town itself and in the surrounding countryside, but during the seventeenth and eighteenth centuries some old industries spread to neighbouring towns. The spinning, weaving, and dyeing of woollens expanded at Roubaix, the production of cotton textiles spread to Tourcoing, linen-making to Armentières, and chemical manufacture to Béthune and Lens. Each of these towns grew rapidly during the nineteenth-century phase of coal-powered mechanization, with Lille continuing to produce textiles and metal goods but also adding a printing industry and an important regional commercial function. In terms of employment, Lille became the most 'balanced' of these towns, combining service functions with manufacturing.

Taking the example of Roubaix in more detail, over 300 textile mills were opened between 1830 and 1850. In the following half-century the town's population grew from 24 000 to 124 000. Given the limited development of public transportation at that time it was necessary to house the new industrial workforce close to its place of work. The courées provided a cheap solution. Tiny industrial cottages were constructed at high densities (350 dwellings per ha) and often without foundations, so that rising damp has been a serious problem. One-third of the courée cottages in Roubaix receive no direct sunlight and another third experience less than two hours' sunlight each day. There are still more than 8500 courée dwellings, housing about 30 000 people in the town. Six thousand courée cottages have their only water supplies from communal taps out in the courtyards, where outdoor lavatories shared by all the households in the courtyard are located. Effluent disposal is rudimentary. The courées of Roubaix, Lille, and other northern cities have been shunned by all who can obtain better accommodation but have become important areas of immigrant housing. It has been estimated that 40 per cent of the courée population in Roubaix is of immigrant origin, and in some courées virtually all families are immigrants.

Probably the worst housing in the whole region is found in the *courées* that were built in the middle years of the nineteenth century in textile-producing towns such as Roubaix. Urban renovation schemes will clear away these slums soon

The second main type of accommodation problem is linked to the housing stock of the coalfield settlements. Houses were constructed close to mines during the nineteenth century and in the early years of the present century. Destruction during both World Wars has meant that large parts of the mining estates have been rebuilt over the last half-century. Yet in spite of relatively recent rebuilding, two serious deficiencies remain; firstly, the lack of internal facilities in the older mining cottages (*corons*); and secondly, the fact that housing sprang up without any associated provision of shops, schools, entertainment facilities, and other services. This deficiency affects both individual mining communities and the coalfield zone as a whole. Stretching from Artois eastwards to Liège, it houses more than 2 million inhabitants but in several sections has no clearly-defined hierarchy of service provision.

Housing types in the coal basins vary considerably Professor T. H. Elkins (1967) reports that '. . . in the coalfield that surrounds the city of Liège, houses are scattered everywhere, joined in irregular snaking corridors along the roads or scattered through the fields on any little track. They have obviously been built singly, by individuals, rarely in groups, almost never alike or the same height. Usually they are set forward to the edge of the pavement, without any garden space in front, but every so often one will be set back behind the general line. The plots on which they were built were evidently very narrow, and the houses occupied the full width, with blank side walls awaiting other houses to join on, which perhaps have never arrived' (p. 48). By contrast, in sections of the coalfield of northern France large housing

Much housing built by colliery authorities in the present century is good for use in the future, but needs interior improvements. Adequate employment, shopping facilities, and other services need to be provided locally

estates (*cités jardins*) were laid out by colliery authorities during the twentieth century. Many of these *cités* provide tolerable and, in some places, fairly good housing conditions, but lack a rational provision of services. Local shopping facilities are often inadequate but the problem has been relieved somewhat by the operation of mobile shops.

Unfortunately the presence of several thousand inhabitants in a mining area does not automatically create a 'town' or guarantee provision of the range of commercial, social, and cultural facilities that one expects to find in an urban settlement. For example, La Louvière (23 000 inhabitants) is sadly lacking in the range of facilities that should be found in the leading settlement of the Centre area (total population of 180 000) of Wallonia. Fierce rivalries between municipalities throughout the problem region do not ease matters, hindering the provision of facilities at key centres to serve sub-regional and local hinterlands.

Environmental degradation

Even broader than the deficiencies of housing and service provision, is the general problem of environmental degradation that has been graphically described as 'urban leprosy'. Slag-heaps,

derelict buildings, poor housing, antiquated road systems, and air- and water-pollution emanating from mines and factories combine to create a very unfavourable impression in many parts of the Nord and southern Belgium. The old image of farmers growing crops or grazing livestock right up to the foot of spoil-heaps is still appropriate in some areas, such as the old Borinage mining zone where 6 per cent of the surface is occupied by tip-heaps. Industrial dereliction and landscape chaos do not adequately reflect the economic potential of the coalfields but for a long time they discouraged industrialists from opening new factories in such dismal environments. Up to a quarter of the volume of some spoil-heaps is composed of combustible materials that might be recovered for use in thermal power stations. Such suggestions have not been greeted favourably by local miners being made redundant by the closure of the pits. However, other types of spoil may be processed for use in cement production or employed as ballast or clinker. Recovery operations and flattening of spoil-heaps are both very expensive, even though reclaimed land may be employed usefully for sports grounds or in a number of other uses that would not suffer too much should subsidence occur. Land-

Slagheaps and miners' housing superimposed on areas of highly-productive farmland that are criss-crossed by railways and main roads characterize the land-use pattern of the northern French coalfield

scaping, tree planting, and designation as public open spaces are cheaper alternatives.

Population problems of the Nord

Population problems in the Franco-Belgian border zone reached serious proportions in post-war years. But these problems are of contrasting character, with rapid population growth continuing in northern France whilst demographic stagnation and decline affect parts of Wallonia.

Partly as a result of poor housing conditions, the infantile mortality rate in the Nord region (26·3 per thousand) is as high as in such under-developed parts of France as the southern Massif Central and Corsica. The proportion of deaths caused by tuberculosis is as high as in the remote and backward areas of rural Brittany. Nevertheless, the Nord forms part of the high birth-rate crescent of northern France, having a crude birth-rate of 19·2 per thousand (1968) which was well in excess of the national average (16·6 per thousand). High birth-rates have given the Nord an atypical age structure and each year push large numbers of young people on to the regional employment market which, as we have seen, has built-in weaknesses. As well as experiencing contraction in certain key economic

sectors, the employment situation of the Nord is aggravated by a lack of local mobility and a general unwillingness of its inhabitants to take jobs in other parts of the region which might necessitate moving house. Between 1962 and 1968 some sections of the countryside of northern France underwent rural depopulation but most urban communities experienced growth. The only notable exceptions were some coalfield settlements which stagnated (for example, Lens) or declined (Bruay-en-Artois) (Table 5). Taking the Nord as a whole, the region's population increased by 0·7 per cent between 1962 and 1968 to reach 3 815 060.

Demographic decline of Wallonia

Demographic conditions are very different in southern Belgium which has undergone serious population loss in recent decades. During the nineteenth century the coal-based economy of southern Belgium was booming, and Flanders was the less-developed part of the country. But since the 1930s the economy and population of the South has stagnated whereas the Flemish population has grown rapidly. The Walloon section of Belgium's population fell from 42 per cent in 1875 to 32 per cent in 1972 (Table 6) and will decline even further in the future.

Conversely, the Flemish North rose to great importance with 56 per cent of Belgians living there in 1972.

This is partly explained by a clear contrast in rates of natural change (Table 7). The Walloon South has moderate birth and death rates, and thus a low rate of natural increase (0·18 per thousand), whilst the Flemish North has a comparable birth rate, a much lower death rate and a rate of natural increase (3·19 per thousand) that is much higher than in Wallonia but less than half that for the Nord region (7·9 per thousand). As in other parts of Western Europe, post-war rates of natural increase declined progressively after the 'baby boom' of the late 1940s and 1950s. In the last decade overall rates of population change in Belgium have displayed a marked contrast between the losses or very slight increases recorded in the *arrondissements* in the Walloon South and particularly buoyant increases in most parts of the Flemish North (Fig. 8). However some old-industrialized parts of Western Flanders possess demographic features that are rather more typical of southern Belgium. Because of contrasting conditions of natural change, Wallonia and the bilingual Brussels region contain an above-average proportion of elderly people and a relative shortage of children (Table 8). Fewer people lived in the central business districts of Brussels and Liège in 1970 than ten years previously, but suburban areas around these cities continued to grow rapidly. The only other urban settlements in Belgium to lose population in the 1960s were in the old-industrial areas of the Borinage, the Centre and around Verviers.

A report by Alfred Sauvy, the eminent French demographer, painted a strikingly dismal picture of the demographic 'asphyxiation' of Wallonia, where population loss was combined with an out-dated economy, poor communications, and a predominance of nineteenth-century housing. However, after World War II immigrant labour was required for work in southern Belgian

TABLE 5
Population changes in major urban areas of the Nord, 1962–8

	1962	1968	Percentage change
Armentières (a)	47 160	50 583	+ 7·3
Arras (c)	62 308	72 128	+15·8
Béthune (b)	142 623	144 678	+ 1·4
Boulogne (a)	90 282	93 103	+ 3·1
Bruay–en–Artois (b)	131 092	126 520	− 3·5
Calais (a)	88 142	94 316	+ 7·0
Denain (b)	123 588	126 740	+ 2·6
Douai (b)	194 146	205 432	+ 5·8
Dunkirk (a)	126 318	143 425	+13·5
Lens (b)	325 072	325 696	+ 0·2
Lille–Roubaix–Tourcoing (a)	821 228	881 439	+ 7·3
Maubeuge (a)	85 105	91 367	+ 7·4
Valenciennes (a)	211 228	223 629	+ 5·9

(a) northern and coastal urban areas; (b) coalfield urban areas; (c) southern urban areas.

TABLE 6
Population changes in Belgium, 1838–1972

	1838	Percentage 1875	1958	1972	Total population, 1972
Walloon South	39	42	34	32	3 180 118
Flemish North	53	47	51	56	5 477 727
Brussels bilingual region	8	11	15	12	1 069 005
Belgium	100	100	100	100	9 726 850

TABLE 7
Natural change in Belgium, 1972

	Birth rate per thousand	Death rate per thousand	Natural change per thousand
Walloon South	13·91	13·73	+ 0·18
Flemish North	13·91	10·72	+ 3·19
Brussels bilingual region	13·13	13·44	− 0·31
Belgium	13·82	12·00	+ 1·82

TABLE 8
Age structure in Belgium, 1972 (per cent)

	0–14 years	15–64 years	65 years and over
Walloon South	22·6	62·7	14·7
Flemish North	24·9	62·9	12·2
Brussels bilingual region	19·3	64·6	16·1
Belgium	23·6	63·0	13·4

Fig. 8. Language Regions and Rates of Population Change in Belgium 1960–70, by *arrondissement*

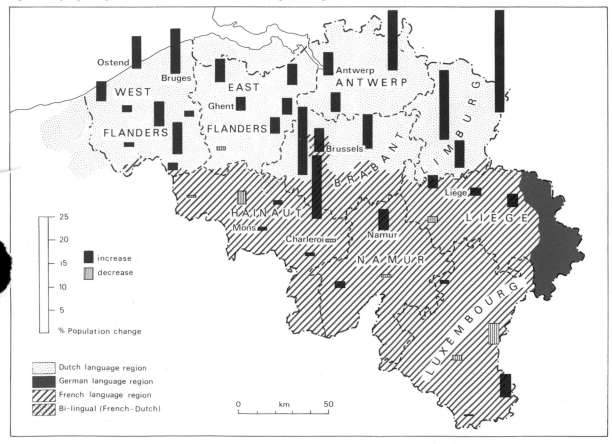

coalmines and other industries that could not be adequately operated by the shrinking local labour force, albeit supplemented by migrants from Flanders. Thus Belgian authorities made recruitment agreements with Italy (1954), Greece (1957), Spain (1958), and Turkey and Morocco (1964), for obtaining supplies of migrant labour. In 1957, 188 500 foreigners were already living in Wallonia and ten years later the figure had risen to 360 000, with immigrants representing over one-tenth of the population of southern Belgium. Without their presence demographic stagnation would have been even more severe. Most male immigrants found employment in mines, metal manufacture, and the construction industry. Women immigrants were employed in domestic service and other service jobs. Reproduction rates of immigrant families are higher than those of Walloon families. However, since the mid-1960s, re-organization of coal-mining and other traditional industries has demanded fewer foreign workers in the South.

Walloons, outnumbered in Belgium, feel even more isolated in the broader context of Benelux which they see as dominated by Dutch (including Flemish) culture and symbolized by the dynamic industrial areas of the Rhine deltalands extending southwards from Rotterdam through Antwerp to the bilingual city of Brussels. This reversal in economic and numerical strength has been of great political significance in Belgium where parliamentary representation is more closely related to the absolute number of voters support-ing particular parties—i.e. to a form of pro-portional representation—than is the case in Britain.

During the 1950s the Walloon South lost 60 000 jobs, in contrast with the creation of 151 000 new ones in Flanders and a further 60 000 in the Brussels area. The same trend continued in the 1960s with Wallonia losing 85 000 jobs in the coal industry, agriculture, steel-making, and other traditional forms of employment. The working population of Wal-lonia declined by 7·0 per cent between 1947 and 1969, falling from 1 183 000 to 1 100 800. This was the opposite of the trend in the Flemish North, which gained 128 000 more jobs, rising from 1 636 000 to 1 765 000 (+ 7·8 per cent), and in the Brussels region, where jobs increased by 61 700, from 562 500 to 624 200 (+ 10·0 per cent). A more detailed distribution of the proportion of the national workforce in each region and province in 1947 and 1969 is given in Table 9.

Until the mid-1960s rates of unemployment were higher in the Flemish North than in Wallonia but then the relationship changed. In 1968 Walloon unemployment rates (6·6 per cent) were considerably higher than the national average (4·8 per cent) and the rates for Flanders (4·5 per cent) and the Brussels area (2·6 per cent). As in northern France, the ranks of the unemployed included large numbers of school leavers as well as mature workers released from declining activities. The net result has been for many Walloons to look for jobs in more dynamic parts of Belgium. This reverses the established pattern of the nineteenth century when the growing industries of the South had attracted Flemish migrants. During the 1960s Wallonia lost over 25 000 residents who moved north-wards. Another solution was for Walloon workers to continue to live in the South but to commute long distances each day to jobs in Brussels, Flanders, or surrounding countries. However the number of Belgian *frontaliers* declined nationally from 66 000 in 1961 to 52 600 in 1967, when 24 000 commuted to work in the Netherlands, 22 600 to France, and smaller numbers to Luxembourg and Federal Germany.

TABLE 9
Percentage share of national workforce by region and province, 1947–69

Region	1947	1969	Province	1947	1969
Walloon South	35·0	31·5	West Flanders	11·1	11·0
Flemish North	48·4	50·6	East Flanders	14·7	14·0
Brussels bilingual region	16·6	17·9	Antwerp	14·5	15·5
			Limburg	4·7	6·0
Belgium	100·0	100·0	Hainaut	14·9	13·2
			Namur	3·8	3·6
Total workforce	3382	3489	Liège	11·9	10·4
(thousands)			Luxembourg	2·2	2·0
			Brabant	22·2	24·3

4 Attempts to Tackle Regional Problems

Regional potential for economic revival

In spite of containing social and economic problems of great magnitude, northern France and neighbouring parts of Belgium display some features that might appear attractive to industrialists and encourage them to install new factories.

First, the problem region occupies a key location in Western Europe, being set between Paris, Brussels, Randstad Holland, and the Rhineland cities of Federal Germany. Over 60 million people live within a 300 km radius drawn from any point along the Lille–Liège axis and this population might be viewed as a potential market for goods manufactured in the Franco-Belgian Border Region. However, old systems of land and water communication would have to be improved before this locational advantage could be exploited to the full.

Second, northern France, Wallonia, and Flanders have long traditions of industrial production, and contain large numbers of people accustomed to factory work. An important legacy of manufacturing expertise, sub-contracting facilities and skills await use by new employers. Each year large numbers of young people come onto the labour market in Flanders and the Nord. They could be usefully absorbed by new industries as might the under-employed female labour force of the mining areas and the men released from declining activities. Retraining would, of course, be a major priority.

Before these latent advantages could be realized two main lines of action needed to be taken. The appropriate government authorities needed to make northern France and neighbouring Belgian areas more 'attractive' to new employers by providing financial inducements for job creation as part of their regional development strategies. Systems of communication also needed to be modernized so that factory operators might take advantage of the favourable possibilities that the 'European' location of the problem region had to offer.

Aid for regional development in France

Once national economies had been restarted after the disruption of World War II, many West European governments became aware of the serious economic and social problems that affected parts of their national territories. In France a package of measures for regional development was introduced in 1955. This included the definition of development areas (*zones critiques*) where large numbers of jobs were being lost from mining, textile production, and other old industries. Direct grants and cheap loans were made available from the Government to help construct new factories, modernize existing ones, and generally to assist the installation of replacement jobs. Auchel-Bruay in the western section of the coalfield of the Pas-de-Calais and the woollen-producing area of Avesnes-Fourmies in south-eastern Nord were selected for help in this early phase. The system of financing industrial development has changed several times since then, with Calais being admitted to the ranks of development areas in 1958. Six years later the definition of industrial conversion zones brought aid to western sections of the coalfield and to textile areas in the Boulonnais and elsewhere in the Pas-de-Calais. In 1972 the system was changed once again, but the coalfield of the Pas-de-Calais still qualified for maximum rates of assistance (up to 25 per cent of total investment for new factories, and 20 per cent for enlarging existing works), along with old industrial areas in north-eastern, central and western France, that also needed replacement jobs (Fig. 9). Other sections of northern France and the whole of the western half of the country qualified for lower rates of assistance. In 1973 maximum rates were extended to areas around Douai and Valenciennes in the Nord. Thus the present scheme for industrial development aims to install new factory jobs in the broad rural West, to create replacement jobs in mining and industrial areas of the North, North-east and Centre of France together with some western cities, and thereby to reduce the stranglehold of Paris on the national economy.

Aid for regional development in Belgium

Regional economic problems had been apparent in Belgium during the 1930s when chemicals, plastics, electronics, and other modern industries were implanted in Flanders as in the Netherlands to the north, whilst at the same time old-established industries in Wallonia started to shed labour. Local authorities tried to encourage the opening of new factories, and special economic councils were set up to study Wallonia in 1945 and Flanders in 1952. Not until 1959 was government action taken to provide financial help for areas with high unemployment rates, important outmigration and out-commuting, and declining traditional industries (Fig. 10). At the same time large investments were made for improving urban conditions in Brussels, in order to make it a truly 'European' city, to extend the port of Antwerp, and to modernize the steel industry of Liège province.

Finance was made available under the Regional Development Act of 1959 to modernize old industries, to introduce replacement jobs in mining, metallurgical, and textile areas, and to open new factories in rural parts of the country. These measures proved insufficient. Long-established industries continued to contract. Old manufacturing areas were not attractive enough in their own right to encourage industrialists to install new factories, nor did the additional jobs that were created keep up with the pace of population growth in the Flemish North or the rate of redundancies in

Wallonia. Thirty criteria—including, amongst others, employment, wage levels, and commuting —were used to define new development areas.

The resultant Regional Development Act of 1966 tried both to encourage industrial revival in declining areas and also to stimulate development in parts of the Flemish North that had already shown their potential for economic advance and employment growth. One quarter of Belgium, accounting for 3·4 million people (one-third of the national population) was covered by the new regulations (Fig. 10). The mining regions of Borinage, Centre, and Campine were included, together with areas of rapid population growth in Flanders and parts of south-eastern Belgium where agricultural jobs were decreasing. Hainaut and other Walloon industrial areas were included because of the importance of their existing housing and industrial premises which might be interpreted optimistically as attractions for new development. Direct grants, low-interest loans, temporary exemption from local taxation, and special incentives for foreign investors were offered to encourage the opening of new factories.

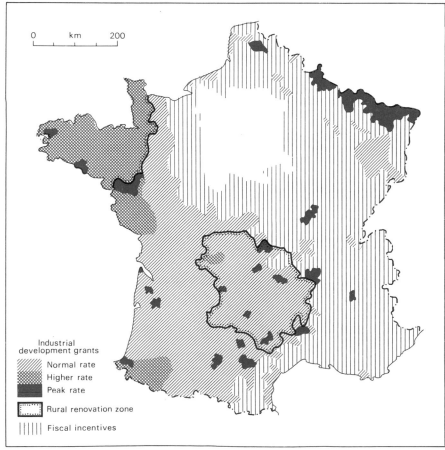

0   km   200

Industrial development grants

Normal rate

Higher rate

Peak rate

Rural renovation zone

Fiscal incentives

In 1970, areas qualifying for financial aid towards industrialization were increased to cover all parts of Belgium except Antwerp and Brussels. However two years later the E.E.C. ruled that this regional-aid law was contrary to Community policy and that a maximum number of twenty-eight districts, rather than forty-one, might qualify for help. By this decision the Commission defended its principle that aid should be granted only to really depressed regions and be used to improve infrastructure rather than act as a permanent support to indu͏͏͏. The Community's aim is to prevent over-gene͏ous state aid in any one country creating unfair competition among industries in the E.E.C. countries. Systems of regional aid in both Belgium and France will be subject to change once again when the common regional policy for the enlarged E.E.C. is eventually decided upon.

Improved communications

Improvements have been made to the existing communications pattern of northern France and Belgium since World War II and some vital new elements have been added. The Nord possessed a very dense canal network which had been completed almost entirely before 1825. Until recently it was burdened by a large number of small locks and shallow canal sections that had been suited to the needs of vessels in the eighteenth and nineteenth centuries but were sadly out-dated after 1945. This pattern was modified by the opening of the Canal du Nord to Paris in 1966 and the creation of a deep-water link between Dunkirk and Valenciennes, with a spur to Lille (Fig. 2). This canal is capable of handling 3000-tonne vessels and already the greater part is operational.

In Belgium the Albert Canal across the Campine watershed was constructed between 1930 and 1939 in order to link industrial Wallonia through Belgian territory with the port of Antwerp for the carriage of iron ore, coal, and other heavy goods, thereby improving the competitiveness of Wallonia vis-à-vis the Flemish North. The 130 km-long Albert Canal is accessible to 2000-tonne vessels and is very heavily used. There are other schemes for water-way deepening. The Meuse is navigable for

Fig. 10. Development Areas in Belgium and Distribution of American Factories (Source: P. Mingret, *loc. cit.*, 1972, page 16)

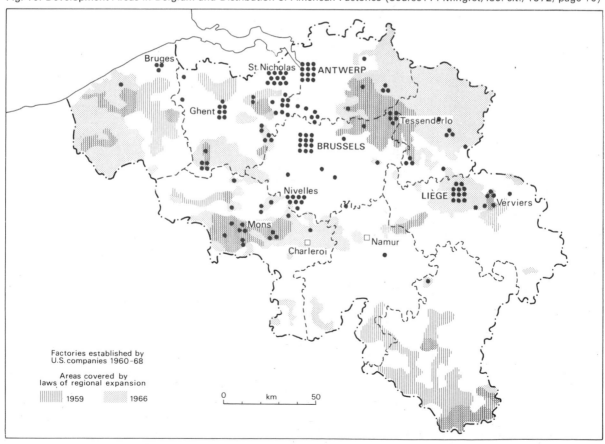

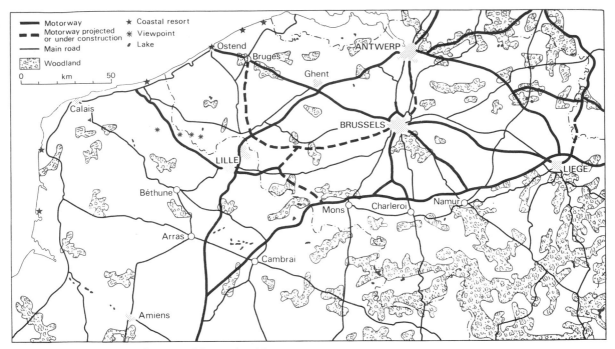

Fig. 11. Road Network and Features of Recreational Importance

vessels of up to 1350 tonnes as far as Givet on the French border but there is no deep-water link into France. The Sambre can take 1350 tonne vessels from Namur to Charleroi, with vessels of this capacity also being able to use the Brussels–Charleroi Canal after the opening of inclined-plane lifts at Ronquières. Upper sections of the Belgian Sambre can only take vessels of under 300 tonnes. The Canal du Centre also has a 300-tonne bottleneck section for some kilometres before reaching a deeper (1350 tonne) section to the west. Ultimately, deep-water links will be required from southern Belgium to the deep French canals that give access to Dunkirk and Paris, but before this can be achieved, long-standing competition between Antwerp and Dunkirk and rivalries over the definition of their appropriate hinterlands, must be worked out.

In northern France and Belgium the mid-nineteenth century railway networks have been modernized extensively, with main-line services being electrified and speeded up since 1950. Lille is now less than two hours away from Paris by train. However some local rail services are still very slow, for example through the backbone of Wallonia from Charleroi to Tournai, via La Louvière and Mons.

The main-road pattern has until recently represented a mixture of highways, built in the eighteenth and nineteenth centuries, and old rural roads that were incorporated in growing urbanized areas over the last 150 years. Road communications were particularly difficult through sections of the coalfields and the old textile towns. To reduce these problems, by-passes and road improvements have been completed in recent years, for example along the *route nationale* 43 through parts of the coalfield of the Pas-de-Calais.

New roads have also been built. The northern motorway from Paris almost reaches the Belgian frontier, with only a small section awaiting completion to the north of Lille (Fig. 11). This motorway joins on to the Belgian network, leading to Ghent, Antwerp, and into the Netherlands. The last section of the eastern spur from the Paris–Lille motorway was opened late in 1972 and links with the Walloon motorway running through industrial south Belgium to Aachen and the Rhinelands. To a certain extent this motorway compensates for the poor passenger train services that operate along the Walloon axis. The city of Liège has motorway connections with Antwerp, Brussels, Ghent and Ostend, and other parts of Wallonia are linked by motorway to Antwerp and Brussels. The Dunkirk–Lille motorway is now also complete and this will soon be joined to the Walloon motorway when a small section in Belgium is built.

Northern France and neighbouring parts of Belgium now have uninterrupted motorway access to major ports and industrial areas throughout north-west Europe, as well as to Paris and Mediterranean France. Further motorways will be constructed in the near future, such as sections of the A 26 linking western parts of the coalfield to the Paris–Lille motorway between 1973 and 1976. In addition, motorways are planned into south-eastern Belgium from Liège and Namur to Arlon and Luxembourg. In the more distant future, the creation of the Channel Tunnel will necessitate major highway improvements to the terminal site near Calais. Possible implications of the Tunnel will be discussed in later paragraphs but they will certainly enhance the 'European' location of the Franco-Belgian Border Region.

Industrial developments in the Nord

During the 1950s and the greater part of the 1960s the Nord region was markedly lacking in modern assembly-type industries. As in Lorraine, the traditional strength of northern France had been in the initial stages of industrial transformation. One might argue, with some justification, that the military vulnerability of both areas had discouraged industrialists from establishing non-essential finishing plants. As recently as the mid-1960s the Lille conurbation and the Nord region as a whole had not shared in the decentralization of factories and offices from Paris that had been engineered as part of French regional-development policies to the benefit of other sections of France, especially the southern and western areas of the Paris Basin. At that stage northern France was not playing its part in producing synthetic textiles, cars, plastics, radio equipment, precision engineering, and consumer goods.

The formation of an industrial development association in the Nord in 1966 heralded a major change in this situation. The association is organized to prospect outside the region to find suitable industrialists who might be interested in moving to the Nord; to direct factory operators to appropriate sites for industrial development; and to facilitate links between industrialists, government bodies awarding financial aid for new factories, and other public services. At the time of its foundation, the association, which represents the regional coal and steel industries, local chambers of commerce, and professional bodies, was acclaimed as the most significant development in northern France since the beginning of the twentieth century. It seems to have lived up to that warm reception. By the beginning of 1974, 39 000 industrial jobs had been created with the help of the association and a further 26 500 were expected to be provided in the future as factories moved towards capacity production. Until 1968 the Essarts estate at Béthune, with its 2000 workers, had been the showplace industrial site heralding the economic conversion of the northern coalfield. Now several industrial corporations are operating factories that will offer up to 8000 jobs each when they are completed.

In 1969 the regional *préfet* reported quite rightly that '. . . the region now faces quite different opportunities from those experienced five years ago when we watched the Nord losing its dynamism while industrial growth forged ahead elsewhere in France'. The late 1960s and early 1970s have seen an important increase in government investment in the form of grants for industrial development in the Nord. For example, in the three years 1964–66 only 3·2 million francs of government aid for industrial growth were devoted to the region, but between 1969 and 1971, 75 grants totalling 181·0 million francs were awarded, and over 20 000 jobs were created. This figure was greater than for any other French planning region over the same period, no more than about 15 000 new jobs being created in Bretagne, Lorraine, or the Pays de la Loire. The change in rate of job creation is indicated by the fact that 109 grants for industrial development were made in the Nord between 1955 and 1971, creating 24 000 new jobs, but five-sixths of these jobs dated from awards in the final three years.

The arrival of the car industry in the Nord
Whilst it is important to stress the number of new jobs created, it is also necessary to emphasize that many, as in cars and plastics, are in sectors that were traditionally absent from the Nord with its nineteenth-century legacy of heavy industrial development. The car industry, entirely absent from the region in 1965, provided almost 10 000 jobs at the beginning of 1973. It has been attracted to northern France by three main factors. Firstly, as we have seen, the Nord is a region with a long industrial tradition, a ready supply of labour (in dire need of employment), and a wide range of expertise and services that might be of value to new industrial enterprises. Secondly, the Nord is in a good position for distributing vehicles to Paris and to neighbouring countries of the Common Market. The motorways to Paris and southern Belgium have provided attractive sites for vehicle and accessory factories, as has the deep-water canal between

Dunkirk and Valenciennes whose banks have been selected for the Peugeot-Renault, Simca, and Renault works. In addition, the dynamic port of Dunkirk offers good facilities for exporting vehicles. Certainly there was a clear link between the completion of the Paris–Lille motorway in 1968 and the decision of the car companies to come to the Nord. The Simca factory at Bouchain occupies a key location at a point where the Paris–Brussels motorway and the Dunkirk–Valenciennes deep-water canal intersect. Thirdly, there is the impact of State financial encouragement for enterprises to move to the Nord and its equally important discouragement for firms to open factories in more immediately attractive areas in the Paris Basin. The large number of young workers coming on to the regional labour market and the contraction of employment in coal, metallurgical, and textile sectors, partly explains the Government's line. Indeed State action alone does much to explain the rapidity of economic change in northern France in under ten years.

The Nord now has 15 per cent of French capacity for car production and is second only to the Paris region in this respect. The nationalized Renault corporation has opened works in a triangular area bounded by Lille, Bruay-en-Artois and Douai. A joint Renault-Peugeot plant at Douvrin produces foundry goods, motor engines, and parts and will employ 7–8000 workers by 1978. The Renault works at Ruitz manufactures gearboxes, and a third plant near Douai assembles vehicles and will employ 7–8000 workers in 1975. Another large assembly works is operated by Simca (Chrysler) at Bouchain, near Valenciennes. In addition, factories for manufacturing car parts have been installed at Etaples (Ducellier corporation, 1500 jobs), Hénin-Liétard (Quillery, 4500 jobs), and Calais (Lucas, 2–300 jobs). Finally, tyre production at Béthune and Lens provides over 1700 jobs and the manufacture of tyre-making machinery accounts for 400 new jobs in Roubaix.

Light industries in the Nord
Among the range of other light industries introduced into the Nord, plastics deserves particular mention. The regional coal authority developed its own carbo-chemicals industry producing plastics and other goods in the early 1960s. Now this trend has been taken up by other firms employing different raw materials and using sites other than those on the coalfield. The Nord, with its car-accessory firms, clothing factories, and other consumer industries, forms an important outlet for locally-produced plastics. Nevertheless, the region contains only about 6 per cent of all workers in the French plastics industry. Its importance derives less from the number of employees involved than from the impact of plastics as a symbol of industrial innovation.

Other light industries include electronics, colour-television assembly, cosmetics, and mail-order activities. A further industrial innovation is the opening at Douai of a branch of the national printing works, which will eventually provide 1000 jobs. The first buildings were completed at the end of 1973. Some of these light industries occupy greenfield sites along main communications axes, but others have been installed in vacant buildings at pitheads or in empty textile mills.

Modernization of old-established industries
Existing industries have modernized their activities in the Nord. Changes in the textile industry are exemplified by the conversion of the old Courtauld works at Calais to the manufacture of modern synthetic fibres. The region's steel industry, despite problems of contraction in the Sambre and Schelde valleys, has important projects for expansion. The Société-Creusot-Loire, employing 3000 men at Les Dunes, will double its production of specialized steels and increase its workforce during the 1970s. The Usinor steel corporation at Dunkirk already has three blast furnaces in operation and employs 7000 men. By the end of 1975 an additional blast furnace—the largest in the world—will be operative and up to 11 000 workers will be employed. Production will rise to 8 million tonnes per annum out of a national total of 31 million tonnes at the end of the Sixth National Plan in 1975. An additional rolling mill will employ 1500 men.

Work has been undertaken by the French Coal Board and local mining authorities to develop alternative forms of employment as a partial compensation for the loss of work in mining. The Bassée industrial estate is an example of colliery-owned land being made available for new factories with financial help from the E.C.S.C. In 1967 the S.O.F.I.R.E.M.* was set up to tackle this task and up to the end of 1971 ten industrial development operations had been completed in the Nord, involving the creation of almost 2000 jobs. Projects that were developed include the manufacture, at Bruay

* Société Financière pour Favoriser l'Industrialisation des Régions Minières.

and Hulluch, of building materials from cinders and schists derived from coal processing; production of prefabricated housing at Violaines; plastics derived from a coal base at Noeux-les-Mines; and carbochemicals at Mazingarbe.

The pattern of industrial development in the Nord

Recent industrial development in the Nord has been primarily to the benefit of the coalfield and coastal areas, with relatively few new activities being installed in the Sambre or Schelde valleys or in the regional conurbation of Lille-Roubaix-Tourcoing. In the western coalfield zone, new industries are being installed on the northern margins of the coal basin and, in the eastern coalfield, industrial sites are being established around Douai and, to a smaller extent, near Valenciennes. The Seclin industrial estate on the motorway south of Lille has attracted firms that have been decentralized from the inner city. Further to the north, Roubaix and Tourcoing have not experienced much in the way of new employment and feelings expressed in recent local elections reflect a sense of abandonment. Industrial development on the coast is linked largely to the Usinor steelworks which began production in 1962. The decision of the Pechiney corporation not to open an aluminium works to the west of Dunkirk because of world over-production of aluminium has been a bitter blow to the employment prospects of the coastal zone, since the works had been expected to employ 1000 workers by the late 1970s with more jobs being provided locally in associated industries.

Industrial development in Belgium

Industrialization has also been achieved in Belgium with the operation of regional development policies since 1959. About 58 250 new factory jobs were created nation-wide up to 1965 and the number of unemployed workers fell from 25 000 to 14 600 over the same period. This reduction was particularly marked in the Flemish North where the number of unemployed dropped from 20 300 to 9000. Regional development measures were particularly valuable in providing work for some of the 150 000 young workers who appeared on the national labour market between 1959 and 1965. Nevertheless, serious pockets of unemployment remained. After 1967 the rate of national economic growth slowed and the number of unemployed rose, this being particularly serious among young people.

Special planning councils were set up in 1968 for the Flemish North, the Walloon South, and the Brussels area, to help co-ordinate regional action within the framework of objectives established for the national economy. During the 1960s, 212·6 billion Belgian francs were invested by the Government for industrial development, but there were important variations in the way the regions were treated (Table 10). Some 58 per cent of the finance was devoted to the Flemish North, where the emphasis was placed on building new factories, and 70 per cent of the new jobs were provided there. This was due to the fact that the main recipients of aid were foreign firms that settled on greenfield sites in the North. But in Wallonia most money was spent on modernizing old industrial installations. Less than one-third of the government finance spent on new industrial premises was devoted to the South. There have, however, been some important industrial innovations in Wallonia, including the Caltex-Chevron oil refinery and petro-chemical complex at Féluy, 20 km north-north-west of Charleroi, which is supplied by pipeline from Rotterdam via Antwerp. Over one-fifth of the total cost of this industrial scheme was met by State grants and low interest rate subsidies.

This pattern of government investment has been paralleled by private investment and Belgium has made a particular effort through an 'open door' policy to attract overseas investors. American finance has been most important in this respect, accounting for 20 per cent of all investments by industrial corporations in the

TABLE 10
Belgian investment for regional industrial development, 1959–69

	Belgian francs (billions)	Total	Percentage New Development	Modernization
Walloon South	84·6	40	31	49
Flemish North	123·4	58	69	47
Brussels bilingual region	4·6	2	0	4
Belgium	212·6	100	100	100

country during the 1960s. Firms based in other countries made smaller but still significant investment in Belgian industry over the same period, for example, Netherlands 14 per cent, Federal Germany 10 per cent, France 9 per cent, and Italy 6 per cent. Half of the new factories established in Belgium during the decade have benefited in some way from American investment. As in the Nord, new factory jobs have been most important in mechanical and electrical engineering, car assembly, plastics, modern branches of textile production, glass, chemicals, and rubber manufacture.

As well as being extremely valuable, American investment in Belgian industry has demonstrated significant locational changes over the past twenty years. In the 1950s and early 1960s American interest was restricted to Brussels and to the Flemish North where town councils, like those of Bruges, Malines and Saint Nicolas, made particular efforts to create new industrial estates and provide facilities to attract industrialists. But since 1965 the Walloon South has also benefited, in response to better publicity regarding the region's resources, its improved transport facilities (especially the motorways giving access to the Rhinelands and to Paris), and the fact that Flemish wage levels rose rapidly in the 1950s and 1960s to approach the traditionally higher salaries of Wallonia. This was partly because of the creation of relatively well-paid jobs in American factories. The attractiveness of a cheap labour force in Flanders is no longer relevant. In fact in 1969 American investment in Wallonia amounted to 9000 million Belgian francs, with only 1300 million Belgian francs being invested in Flanders. Most of the American-financed factories employ fewer than one hundred workers each, but there are some exceptions, notably the General Motors car-assembly plant (6700 workers) and the Ford tractor plant (2500 employees) on greenfield sites near Antwerp.

The pattern of American-financed factories established in Belgium between 1960 and 1968 has been plotted by Paul Mingret (Fig. 10) who showed that in Flanders their coincidence with official development areas was slight. Main lines of communication and large cities proved more attractive sites for investment. By contrast, there was much greater correspondence with development areas in the Walloon South. The Antwerp–Brussels–Ghent growth axis stands out as a major focus of new factories, with a smaller concentration at Tessenderlo which has good transport facilities in the form of the Albert

Canal and the Antwerp–Liège motorway. In Wallonia, three main areas of American industrial investment emerge. The first is around Liège with an easterly extension at Verviers. The second zone is rather more dispersed between the rival coalfield towns of the Borinage and the Centre. (Case examples from Liège and the Borinage will be examined later.) The third Walloon focus is at Nivelles which has good road communications with the capital and really forms an extension of the Antwerp–Brussels axis to the south of the cultural divide. In Mingret's words '. . . it appears that in the last few years Belgium has undergone profound changes in its regional equilibrium with, in the industrial field, the saturation of Flanders and, by contrast, the very clear regrowth of Wallonia' (1972, p. 15).

These achievements represent simply a beginning in the long and difficult task of revitalizing the lagging economy of the South. Striking inter-regional differences emerge in the pattern of the 280 110 new industrial jobs created in Belgium between 1959 and 1970. Wallonia, with 32 per cent of the national population, received only 29 per cent of the new manufacturing jobs, and Brussels, with 12 per cent of the population, only 2 per cent of new factory jobs. By contrast, Flanders fared very well, with 68 per cent of the new jobs but only 56 per cent of the population. At a finer scale, the provinces of Antwerp (20 per cent of new jobs), West Flanders (14 per cent), East Flanders (17 per cent), and Limburg (12 per cent), were particularly attractive to industrialists (Fig. 12).

Criticisms of regional development

Criticisms of the industrial emphasis in regional development policies have been voiced in both northern France and Belgium. Professor Sporck has argued that southern Belgium (and the same applies to northern France) has been over-reliant on mining and manufacturing in the past, hence schemes for the future well-being of these areas should ensure the provision of service jobs, for it is this sector that is currently growing most rapidly in Western Europe, with manufacturing jobs stabilizing or declining in importance. In a similar vein the O.E.C.D.* has argued that in Belgium manufacturing is not, or should not be, the vocation of every region. Some are more suited to tourism, others to agriculture, forestry, or public service. Regional

* Organization for European Co-operation and Development.

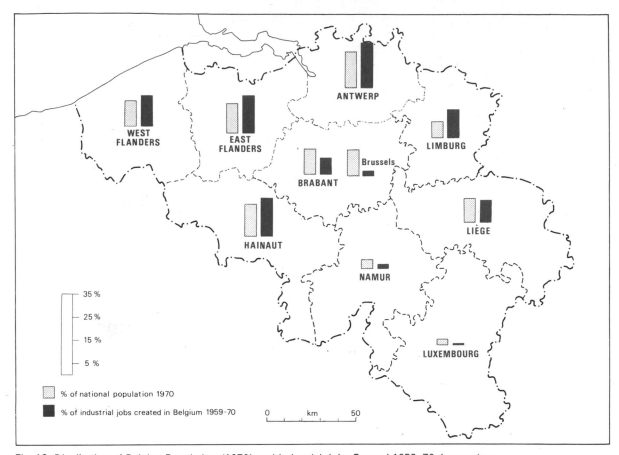

Fig. 12. Distribution of Belgian Population (1970) and Industrial Jobs Created 1959–70, by province

development policies need to be broad enough to embrace all these objectives.

It is true, of course, that new 'tertiary' and 'quaternary' jobs have been created in some parts of the Franco-Belgian Border Region. The Lille metropolis has already received major State-directed educational establishments for training civil servants, architects, and financial specialists. French planners seek to encourage further decentralization of training centres and major offices in sectors such as banking and insurance, to strengthen the decision-making role of northern France. Financial aid for developing tertiary activities had previously been restricted to Lille but is now available to help other parts of the Nord. In southern Belgium the tertiary functions of Liège and some other large towns have been strengthened in recent years with, for example, higher-education facilities being installed at Mons. But office development in the cities of northern France and southern Belgium is hampered by their proximity to Paris and Brussels which have absorbed the lion's share of tertiary and quater-

nary growth in the last two decades. The example of Brussels is particularly striking in this respect.

The growth of Brussels as a 'European' city
The bilingual Brussels region has a population of 1·1 millions, but the urban area extends beyond the bilingual zone and contains 1·5 million residents, roughly 15 per cent of the national total. The city was chosen by the Dukes of Brabant for their administrative centre and, as national capital of the Kingdom of the Belgians since the 1830s, Brussels has acquired an inflated proportion of the nation's professional people. Now it contains, for example, 20 per cent of all doctors and 37 per cent of lawyers in the country. The employment structure of Brussels is orientated towards tertiary activities, with banking and commerce employing 25 per cent of the workforce, miscellaneous services 30 per cent, and transport and communications 8 per cent. This last figure reflects the import-ance of Brussels as an international focus of air and rail communication. The remaining 37

per cent of the workforce is employed in manufacturing.

In the last two decades, Brussels has increasingly become a 'European' capital. Some 41 million foreigners visited the Brussels World Fair in 1958 and in the same year the city became the headquarters of the European Economic Community and the Euratom organization. Nine years later the headquarters of the North Atlantic Treaty Organization were transferred from Paris to a site outside Brussels. Now more than 5000 Eurocrats and their families live in the city. Running parallel with this rise in administrative activities, Brussels has experienced an important property boom, with massive new office blocks being built in central parts of the city where commercial uses of land are replacing housing. The local resident population has declined as a result.

Brussels is also the major focus for migrants leaving other parts of Belgium. Over the past two decades an average of 15 000 provincials moved each year to live in Greater Brussels. Suburban development has been most extensive to the south and south-east of the city centre with housing spreading into rural parts of the Brabant plateau where farms are large and suitable for block purchase and conversion into housing estates. This southward extension of suburban growth also reflects the fact that Walloon migrants to the capital prefer to live in French-speaking areas where their children will be taught in French. By contrast, suburbanization is more restricted over the area of small farms to the west and the market-gardening zones in Flemish-speaking territory to the north and east. This imbalance in suburban growth is also related to the fact that the majority of daily commuters into Brussels come from Flanders. One-third of the 600 000 workers with jobs in Brussels *arrondissement* commute from beyond the area. Eighty per cent of these travellers come from the Flemish North, but the capital's daily commuting hinterland covers 85 per cent of Belgian *communes* with workers taking advantage of cheap rail tickets and the provision of improved train services to Brussels over the last twenty years.

The European Economic Commission's Berlaymont Building symbolizes the role of Brussels as a 'European' capital and represents part of the important construction of office blocks that has taken place in the last few years

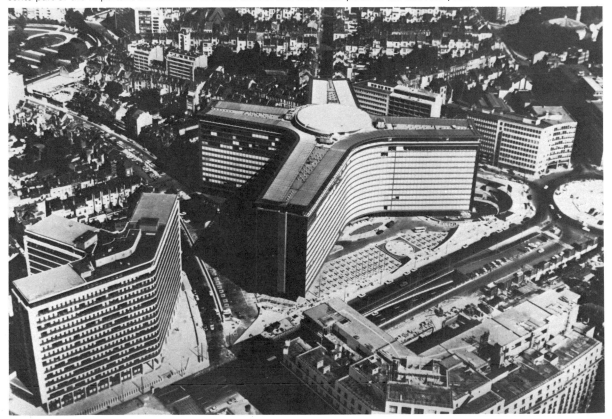

5 Sub-regional Problems

The impact of schemes for regional development varies greatly from area to area and from town to town in the Franco-Belgian Border Region. It is scarcely possible to do justice to all the achievements that have been accomplished or to the problems that still face all parts of the region. Instead, four distinctive sub-regions have been selected for examination in more detail; the Channel Ports of the Nord, the Central Urban Area, the Borinage, and the Province of Liège.

The Channel ports of the Nord

The town of Dunkirk (143 000 inhabitants in 1968) experienced significant growth of population and expansion of port facilities during the 1960s, but it is still very much the poor relation of its Belgian rival, Greater Antwerp, with a population of 673 000. Port installations at Dunkirk have been enlarged over the last decade and the port area extended westwards across a stretch of reclaimed land (Fig. 13). New docks have been excavated to take ore-carriers supplying the Usinor steelworks, and special facilities provided for unloading crude oil destined for the local B.P. refinery and the A.N.T.A.R. refinery 110 km inland at Valenciennes. In terms of cargo handled, Dunkirk now ranks as the third maritime port in France, dealing with more than 25 million tonnes in 1971, of which 8·9 million tonnes were accounted for by oil. In the French context it comes well behind Marseille (75 million tonnes) and Le Havre (60 million tonnes) and is outstripped at a Continental scale by Rotterdam (230 million tonnes), Antwerp (74 million tonnes), Genoa (57 million tonnes) and Hamburg (45 million tonnes). During 1973 Dunkirk's cargo exceeded 31 million tonnes.

Work is underway on constructing an outport for Dunkirk to take 450 000-tonne vessels by the end of 1975. The outport will incorporate a 3 km long tidal basin to be equipped with oil terminals. The western side of the outport will be occupied by industrial premises and the eastern section used for container handling and other shipping activities. In the more distant future, the deep channels off Dunkirk and Calais offer the possibility of affording docking facilities for 500 000-tonne vessels, for example through construction of an offshore island harbour.

Certainly there is abundant land for industrial development along the coastline of northern France. Already construction has started on a cement works and a 6 million tonne oil refinery at Mardyck. Both should be in operation during 1974. But such development raises the threat of environmental degradation and a reduction in the attractiveness of this stretch of coast for tourism. Industrial schemes must be carefully planned in the future.

Forty kilometres along the coast from Dunkirk, the town of Calais (94 300 in 1968) has experienced a chequered economic career since the beginning of the century. The old-established lace industry declined in importance before 1914 but new forms of employment (chemicals, metallurgy, and paper-making) were introduced at that stage and in the inter-war years when Courtaulds started the manufacture of artificial fibres in the town. Calais suffered greatly during World War II when half of the built-up area was damaged and a quarter of the town totally destroyed. Reconstruction was the first post-war objective, but employment problems remained serious, with Calais qualifying for financial assistance for industrial development as early as 1958. These measures have been quite effective with newly-attracted industries including the manufacture of clothing and electrical equipment for cars.

The Channel Tunnel will form a vital new link between the Franco-Belgian Border Region and the British Isles. The Tunnel will be to the advantage of Calais since the site for the eastern terminal has been designated at Coquelles only a few kilometres from the town centre. The idea of a Channel Tunnel dates back at least as far as 1810 when proposals were drawn up for Napoleon. The mid-nineteenth century witnessed a host of ideas for bridges and tunnels. Test boreholes were put down, but that was all. The Channel Tunnel Study Group combining British, French, and American interests was not set up until 1958, and the Anglo-French agreement to go ahead with the scheme was signed as recently as November 1973. A large area has been set aside west of Calais to accommodate road and rail terminals, offices, industry, and warehousing. Port of Calais authorities estimate that two-thirds of existing traffic, comprising

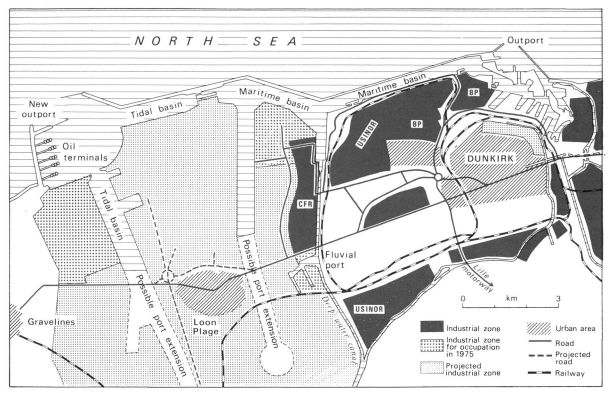

Fig. 13. Port of Dunkirk

roll-on/roll-off passenger and freight services across the Channel, may be liable to diversion to the Tunnel, but it will not take over the handling of large bulk cargoes. The town of Calais expects to obtain considerable advantages from construction of the Tunnel. Local employment opportunities will be increased. Communications will be improved and will act as a stimulus to tourism along the coast, especially in the Boulonnais area to the south. Calais' authorities also look enthusiastically to the possibility of attracting more British industrialists to open factories in their town. Ten are operating there already.

When constructed, the Channel Tunnel will handle special trains on which cars, lorries and passengers will be loaded. Land access to the Tunnel will be improved and this will involve electrification of the Calais–Paris rail service and the construction of a motorway between the port and the Paris-Lille motorway. It is, of course, impossible to gauge the precise implications of the Channel Tunnel on the Franco-Belgian Border Region but it can be safely suggested that it will strengthen the economic and demographic expansion of the coastal zone and will foster the implantation of new forms of industry in the western part of the Nord region,

especially along the link to the Paris motorway where it crosses the coalfield zone with its abundant supplies of labour. Such a development inland from Calais would help to redress the economic balance between the relatively less-developed western part of the Nord and the more urbanized central section of the region. Whilst benefiting western areas, such developments would add to the problems of the inland towns as they attempt to recruit new forms of employment to replace jobs lost in old-established activities.

The central urban area of the Nord

The central urban area may be divided into two parts. To the north is found the metropolitan conurbation of Lille-Roubaix-Tourcoing with a population of 881 400 (1968) and an important heritage of textile manufacture. To the south are the coalfield (perhaps more accurately ex-coal-field) settlements containing in all about one million inhabitants. Each settlement in these two areas experiences its own distinctive combination of social and economic problems, but these may be subsumed under the general heading of 'making do and mending', in other words, of improving the urban facilities of these towns to meet current and future needs.

Plans for this central urban area place great emphasis on the preservation of green wedges to prevent further coalescence between existing built-up areas and between these and the new housing estates that are planned for the remainder of the century (Fig. 14). These inland urban areas are being viewed increasingly as parts of a single sub-region that needs to be managed in an integrated fashion but without direct reference to neighbouring areas in Belgium.

Lille, Roubaix, Tourcoing, and 84 surrounding *communes*, have joined together to form the 'urban community' of greater Lille so that planning problems may be tackled on a broad basis without undue reference to a highly fragmented administrative structure. The inner parts of the three main towns of the 'urban community' have experienced major urban renovation schemes in the past two decades, with many *courées* and other forms of nineteenth-century industrial housing being swept away and replaced by modern residences. As in other urban renovation schemes, the social implications of rehousing are considerable, with old communities

Fig. 14. Proposed Strategy for the Central Urban Areas of the Nord, 1985–2000 (Source: Agence d'Urbanisme de la Communauté Urbaine de Lille, 'La Métropole du Nord' *Urbanisme*, 134–5, 1973, p. 99)

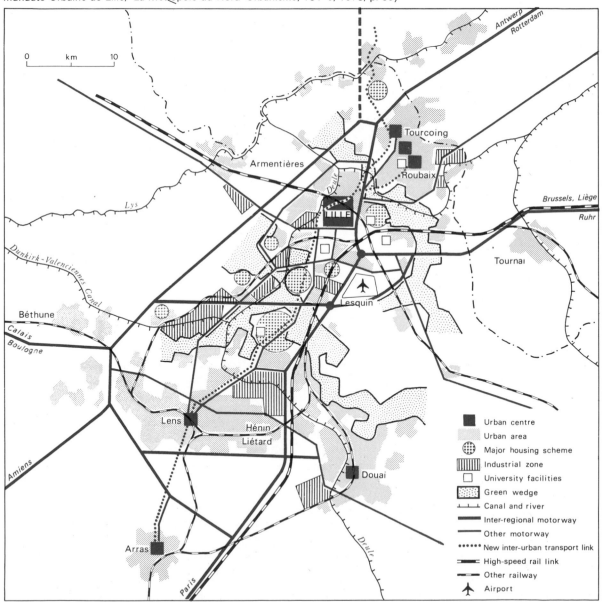

Fig. 15. Planned Structure of Lille-Est New Town

being split up as working-class residents are rehoused on out-of-town housing estates. But two particular elements in the redevelopment of Lille merit out attention.

The first of these is the new commercial centre being built in the redevelopment area close to the central railway station. By 1985 the centre will provide over 530 000 m² of floor-space for shops, offices, housing, and cultural facilities to serve the inner part of the Nord region. The centre will generate 20 000 jobs and will have more than 10 000 parking spaces. Lille is in an unusual location, having its 'natural' hinterland truncated by the international boundary 15 km away. But this is very much a 'permeable frontier' with the commercial facilities of Greater Lille being used by Belgian residents, and French families using the Belgian countryside for recreation.

The second major development involves the new town of Lille-Est (sometimes called Ville-neuve-d'Ascq) which is being constructed 7 km east of Lille, from which it is separated by a small stretch of agricultural land (Fig. 15). Already the Science Faculty of Lille University has moved to its new campus at Annappes, inside the new-town perimeter. This will be followed by the Arts and Social Science Faculty which will move to nearby Flers in 1974. The whole education complex will form an important part of the new town which will house 120 000 residents and 40 000 students by 1985. The former figure will include 30 000 residents who live in villages and small towns inside the designated area, and 90 000 new residents. In fact, the new town will be equipped with commercial, entertainment, and other facilities for a rather larger population and will serve 60 000 additional residents in surrounding settlements. As well as forming an educational focus, providing housing facilities to take some of the overspill resulting from urban renovation in central Lille, and accommodating some of the sub-region's future population growth, the new town will also provide a range of recreational facilities that is sadly absent from the Nord at present. It will include a sports centre based on a 30 000 seat stadium. Lille-Est will be linked to the centre of Lille by the 'VAL' (Véhicules Automatiques Légers) automatic transportation system which will be guided and operated entirely without personnel in stations or trains. Eight stations will give access to the 17 km-long system that will handle up to 6000 passengers an hour. Construction is scheduled for completion in November 1974.

The urban problems of the coalfield are different from those of the northern textile towns. The mining zone was developed in a piecemeal fashion in the nineteenth and early twentieth centuries around the mines of a large number of separate companies. Many settlements grew up without necessary administrative, commercial and recreational facilities. Now one of the main tasks in replanning the coalfield is to build up a rational settlement hierarchy with adequate facilities to match the replacement employment opportunities that are being installed on industrial estates close to Béthune, Bruay-en-Artois, Lens, Hénin-Liétard, and other towns. These new jobs are vital not only for ex-miners and other male workers but also for members of the female labour force who used to commute to work in the northern textile towns where large numbers of jobs have been lost in recent years.

The Nord Coal Board owns 125 000 dwellings on 690 estates, which together house about 450 000 people. It has been estimated that almost 90 per cent of these dwellings represent viable units for future use and therefore merit renovation and improvement. Already a start has been made in redeveloping 500 houses, mostly semi-detached, in the Cité-des-Aviateurs close to Bruay-en-Artois. The ground plan of the estate has been modified by demolishing some houses to create spaces for tree-planting and establishing open spaces and *petanque* greens. Small public parks have been inserted and parking places and garages provided. The houses themselves have been modernized, with inside lavatories and better kitchen facilities. Many more operations of this kind will be essential to improve the housing stock of the

French and Belgian coalfields now that coal mining is no longer a leading form of employment and the settlement pattern of the coal basins has almost completely lost its functional *raison d'être*. Already the two hundred slag heaps in the Nord region have been studied by experts from the Ministry of Culture who have prepared plans for flattening some, landscaping others, and retaining a few as examples of industrial archaeology.

Planners insist that settlements in the two zones that make up the central Nord sub-region need to be bound together more effectively. Motorway construction and further improvement of main roads linking Lille and the coalfield will help achieve this aim, but it has also been suggested that S.N.C.F. and colliery rail lines might be used to operate a fast and frequent inter-urban train service (METRONOR). Similar problems of employment, environment, and communications are encountered in the other coal basins of the Franco-Belgian Border Region.

The Borinage

The Borinage is an urbanized mining area along the Haine valley which is entrenched into surrounding plateaux for almost 20 km between the French frontier and the city of Mons. In addition to coal, the area contains other mineral resources which include pottery-clays, quartzites, chalk, and sand. The coalfield enjoyed its heyday in the eighteenth and nineteenth centuries, but its location soon became something of an international *cul-de-sac*. Establishment of the northern boundary of France in 1815 cut off the Walloon coal basins from their earlier markets in northern France. Fifteen years later the detachment of Belgium from the Netherlands reduced Wallonia's guaranteed market for coal once again. The French imposed dues on navigation from Belgium into northern France and refused to allow canal links to be deepened, thereby protecting domestic coal producers from competition from Wallonia. The Belgian reaction was to establish a wholly Belgian waterway between the Borinage and the Schelde, but this route involved a large number of locks. However, the Borinage is now served by canal links to the Charleroi–Brussels Canal via the Canal du Centre through Mons and La Louvière.

Unlike many other mining areas in the Franco-Belgian problem region, the Borinage did not develop a steel industry but simply concentrated on coal extraction. A suitable site for a steelworks was not immediately obvious in the Haine valley and during the nineteenth century adequate profits could be derived from coal sales. By contrast, the French encouraged Belgian industrialists to invest in factories in northern France. This helps to explain the development of the French steelworks at Maubeuge, 20 km to the south of Mons, which employs a labour force that is partially made up of Belgian *frontaliers*.

Peak coal production of 5·9 million tonnes from the Borinage was achieved in 1927. A quarter of a century later, more than half the area's male workers were still in coal-mining. Foundry work, glass and pottery manufacture, shoe-making, cable production and light engineering provided smaller additional sources of work but in the 1940s and 1950s the glassworks closed and the shoe industry faced severe competition from lower-cost manufacturers in Italy and the Netherlands. The period of inflated demand for Borinage coal in the post-war reconstruction phase was short and the area was soon recognized as a high-cost producer with difficult geological conditions, declining reserves, and poor mining facilities, by comparison with the Campine, the Ruhr, Dutch Limburg, and even northern France. However, the problem of the coal mines was not faced immediately. Discriminatory rail freights worked against Ruhr coal and to the advantage of Belgian supplies in Wallonia. Campine coal prices were pegged high and the Borinage had the advantage of proximity for supplying the steel industry of Charleroi. The Belgian Government subsidized the local coal industry to reduce unemployment and the E.C.S.C. fixed price levels to protect the Borinage. But by the end of the 1950s, imports of American coal were clearly cheaper than local coal which was selling badly. A reorganization programme started, involving a reduction of production, amalgamation of mines, and the release of half the mining workforce. Other local industries were shedding labour at the same time.

Strikes, riots, and protest marches resulted, but 'rationalization' of the coal industry continued. More pits were closed and mining became gradually focused on pits in predominantly rural areas north of the river Haine away from the old mining areas to the south, which housed four-fifths of the area's population. Between 1950 and 1962 the number of people working in the Borinage fell by one-third from 57 400 to 38 400 and in the period 1958–62, 15 600 miners were released. Now only 1500 men are employed in a single mine by comparison with a mining force of 24 000 in 1956. The E.C.S.C. provided 12 months' full pay for miners after their discharge and helped meet costs of retraining and removal of ex-miners to areas that had job vacancies. Loans totalling £5 million were made by the E.C.S.C. to aid the Borinage and neighbouring Centre area. Many miners moved house to Brussels, Antwerp, and elsewhere in Flanders. Some immigrant miners returned home and a number of Borains took advantage of cheap season tickets on fast electrified rail lines from Mons to Brussels for long-distance daily commuting. Now 10 000 Borains commute to work in Charleroi, the Centre area, Brussels, and Valenciennes. This has helped provide employment but ease of access to the well-paid office jobs of Brussels may be seen as something of a 'drain' on the educated workforce of the Borinage.

New local sources of employment were needed urgently, but wage rates in the Borinage were high, labour was militant, and many local industrialists were not innovative in outlook. The idea of making use of old mine sites for the installation of new factories has encountered serious problems. Access to old colliery buildings is often poor and land near the pits is frequently honeycombed with workings. Mining companies still own land and buildings when mining ceases and often remain in occupation for a few years to allow equipment to be moved out. Greenfield sites are more attractive. However progress has been made in flattening and landscaping spoil-heaps. Local authorities are now contemplating the purchase of one of the last sets of winding gear to stand as a memorial to the mining history of the Borinage.

The main hopes for the area have been pinned on the Ghlin-Baudour industrial estate located close to the Walloon motorway and on both banks of the Nimy–Blaton Canal which was deepened in 1964 to take 1350 tonne vessels. The Borinage was given development area status in 1959 and was thus entitled to financial assistance for factory building. The initial response was poor. Only 150 jobs were created during the first two years of the estate's existence, with 12 000 miners being made redundant over the same period. But since then efforts have been made to attract investment from the United States and from other countries. New factories sited on the estate manufacture paper, rubber, metal parts, cement, clothing, and beer. Not all the industrial schemes for the Borinage have proved successful but, by 1973, 8000 manufacturing jobs had been provided in

48 factories built in the area since 1960. The most important of these is an American plant producing aluminium sheet with a payroll of more than 1000. These are not all extra jobs since other old-established works were closed over the same period. Projects for industrial expansion in the future include an American firm which manufactures carton-packaging, a German telecommunications company which plans to increase its local workforce from 300 to 3000, and a Dutch chemical firm with 150 workers which envisages much larger numbers. In addition, new service jobs have eased the employment problems of the Borinage. Indeed, by the mid-1960s the most severe unemployment had passed. The future of the Borinage looks much more hopeful than its immediate past.

Liège province

Despite its long industrial history the city of Liège experienced problems of labour redundancies from traditional forms of employment in the 1950s and 1960s. The employed population of the province fell by 5·4 per cent between 1960 and 1968, whilst in Belgium as a whole it increased by 11·6 per cent. Numbers in agricultural jobs declined rapidly. After a peak output of 6·0 million tonnes in 1906, coal production in the Liège basin fell from 3·8 million tonnes to 1·3 million tonnes during the 1960s (a drop of 63 per cent), whilst national coal production declined by only 27 per cent. Large numbers of miners were released and by 1981 it is likely that all mines in the Liège basin will have closed. Old manufacturing industries such as steel and textiles, are employing fewer workers with, for example, 5000 jobs being lost in the textile mills of Verviers during the 1960s. But set against this picture of economic decline, the Liège area offers a number of important attractions that may be capitalized for future growth.

The city is in the midst of a densely-populated part of north-west Europe and has good road links to the rest of Belgium, France, Federal Germany and the Netherlands. When the motorway programme is complete, Liège will be the second largest motorway junction in Europe, after Milan. Electrified railways and deep waterways provide other important connections, with the Albert Canal to Antwerp planned for deepening to take 9000 tonne vessels in the future. Abundant supplies of water are available from the Meuse and supplies of pure water for special industrial use are provided in the Vesdre valley. Electrical energy is available from steam-generating power stations, the nuclear-power station at Tihange, and the hydro-electric works at Coo. In addition, the province has an important industrial tradition, involving a skilled workforce and numerous small trades available for sub-contracting work. As a university city, Liège offers important facilities for higher education and research.

In order to exploit these and other attractive features, a company for the industrial development of Liège province was set up in 1961, uniting the efforts of local authorities and major employers in the area. Industrial estates have been laid out along motorways and major waterways, especially the Meuse and the Albert Canal. These estates vary in size from 50 ha to over 250 ha. For example, the Chertal estate downstream from Liège has been extended from 160 ha to 370 ha and is the site of a new steelworks. Roads and other facilities are being provided on the estate by the provincial development company.

The best-known industrial estate near Liège is Hauts-Sarts, which was designated in 1958 as the first experimental site for factory construction in the province (Fig. 16). The first plot of land was sold in 1964 and the first factory started production in the following year. Supplies of natural gas from the Netherlands were piped to Hauts-Sarts in 1967. Now the original 185 ha are almost entirely occupied. Proposals exist for extending the estate to 490 ha and some additional areas have already been equipped. Twenty-seven firms have been installed, employing a total of 4000 workers. Foreign companies and firms combining Belgian and overseas capital have been particularly important, accounting for 85 per cent of the jobs provided and 90 per cent of the investment at Hauts-Sarts. Uniroyal-Englebert, with American backing, is the largest industrial unit on the estate, employing about 1600 workers in the manufacture of brake linings and tyres, and producing more than 11 000 tyres each day. Almost all the Belgian firms installed at Hauts-Sarts have been decentralized from central Liège and Herstal. Thus not all the industrial jobs that have been provided are additions to the province's employment total. Some are direct replacements for jobs that have been transferred from old-industrial areas.

American firms have been very important in the development of each of the estates around Liège, with the American Brake Shoe Company, Armco Steel, Pittsburgh Steel, and the Westinghouse Corporation, being represented, together with firms producing fibreglass, pharmaceutical

Fig. 16. Industrial Zones and Communications on the Northern Edge of Liège (Source: J. A. Sporck, *loc. cit.*, 1970, p. 59)

goods, and other products. During the 1960s, 10 700 industrial jobs were created in Liège province, of which 9000 were provided by 59 firms installed on new industrial estates. The significance of Hauts-Sarts in the total picture can be readily appreciated. But more needs to be done, and, as in the other old-industrial areas, the service role of Liège needs to be strengthened.

In addition to providing new jobs, the Liège conurbation, with over 630 000 inhabitants, still has to overcome two major problems. The first is the need to remove the worst legacies of nineteenth and early-twentieth century industrialization: the intermixture of slum housing, tip-heaps, old-industrial buildings, and polluted air and water. Like other industrial cities, Liège forms an urban heat island. Air pollution is most concentrated in the city centre and in the steel-making basin of Seraing. But pollution from industrial sources is now less severe than it was twenty years ago. Gilchrist-Thomas steelworks, which spew out gas, smoke, and dust, are being replaced by oxygen steelworks with efficient filters. Collieries are being closed down. Coal-burning locomotives have been replaced, and new techniques of metal re-

fining cause less pollution than their predecessors. Nevertheless new problems of air pollution derive from increased car ownership and the use of oil-fired central heating. Water pollution is reaching serious levels, especially along some sections of the lower Vesdre and the Meuse. The solution to this problem is not to be found at the local level but requires efficient effluent-treatment plant to be installed throughout the river basins.

The second major problem affecting the Liège urban area involves the provision of adequate shopping facilities and other services for the 350 000 residents of the outer suburbs which grew during the nineteenth and present centuries. Five major service centres have been designated, each to be equipped with services to cater for the needs of 50–70 000 residents, and five smaller centres will also be developed. The Liège urban region thus displays a fundamental contrast between its inner areas, with their legacy of past industrialization, economic contraction, and loss of resident population, and the dynamic outer suburbs with new housing areas, hypermarkets, and modern industrial estates enjoying links to the motorway network.

6 The Region in the Future

The Franco-Belgian Border Region has experienced serious social and economic problems in the last quarter of a century but important action has been taken since the mid-1960s to provide jobs to replace those that were lost, to improve housing, and to modernize communications. Each of these objectives will demand attention in future years since farm-workers will continue to leave the land, old sources of industrial employment will disappear or be mechanized and thus require fewer workers, and coal-mining may even be terminated by the mid-1980s. It is not inconceivable, however, that the energy crisis may prolong the economic life of some pits. Nevertheless, coal extraction in the future will become increasingly mechanized and will not be a large employer of labour. Colliery settlements and textile towns will need to be remodelled for future needs. However, greater proportions of replacement jobs will have to be provided in the service sector rather than in manufacturing industry since it is the former

that appear to offer the greater potential for growth in the future.

Motorways, industrial estates, housing schemes, new towns, and other features of modern urban civilization are nibbling away the remaining stretches of countryside in what is already one of the most densely-populated and urbanized parts of Europe. Efficient planning is required to avoid a repetition of the land-use chaos that degraded many industrial and mining districts of northern France and Belgium prior to World War II. Conservation of rural land is necessary for two main reasons.

Firstly, the region contains some of the richest farmland on the Continent and is a very intensive producer of a wide range of agricultural goods (Fig. 17). For example, the Nord region covers only 2 per cent of the French land surface but 5 per cent of French milk, 6 per cent of barley, 8 per cent of wheat, 10 per cent of potatoes and nearly 20 per cent of sugar beet are produced there. Agricultural yields are among the highest

Fig. 17. Land Use (Source: *World Atlas of Agriculture*, Istituto Geografico De Agostini, Novara, 1969, plates 4 and 5, Central and North-Western Europe)

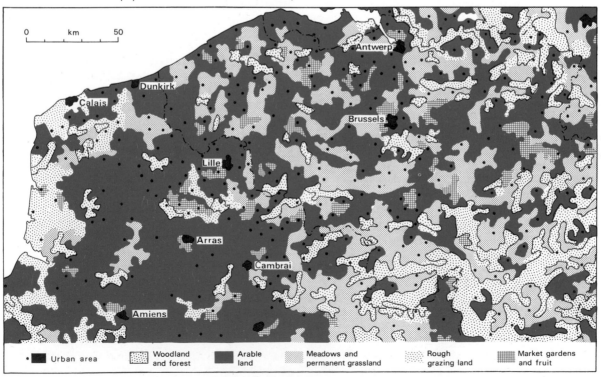

| | Urban area | Woodland and forest | Arable land | Meadows and permanent grassland | Rough grazing land | Market gardens and fruit |

in France. Conditions are comparable in neighbouring parts of Belgium. This valuable land resource needs to be safeguarded for rational exploitation in the future rather than being smothered by concrete or tarmac. Planners envisage the agricultural future of the region in terms of placing more emphasis on high-quality products such as market-garden crops, even though there will continue to be considerable local variation in farming specialization between the various 'natural regions' of the border zone.

Secondly, the countryside will be used increasingly in the future for recreation by the region's car-owning population. The 'natural' recreation potential of Flanders is not high but there are a number of important wooded sites, water surfaces, viewpoints, and historic towns, that need to be protected and managed sympathetically for leisure use (Fig. 11). Already a 10 000 ha regional nature park at Saint-Amand-Raismes, close to Valenciennes, has been equipped for recreational use. Some of the damp valleys of the interior of the region, such as the Scarpe and the Sensée, are being developed as multi-purpose recreation-cum-water storage areas to serve the cities of the central urban area of the Nord. They also perform the subsidiary function of green wedges to prevent the coalescence of urban areas. The Channel coast of northern France and Belgium has a number of holiday resorts and also a series of less-developed sites that are used for recreation. Care must be taken to control the spread of urban and industrial development along the coast so that the landscape and other resources of these areas may be conserved. Planners in the Nord are devising recreation schemes that respect local ecological conditions along their stretch of coastline, channelling intensive recreational uses to areas that will be able to withstand pressure and controlling access to stretches with fragile ecosystems.

The uplands of the Ardennes in Wallonia and their extension southwards into the Avesnois are very attractive weekend recreation areas for the inhabitants of northern France, Belgium and neighbouring countries. Motorway construction has made this area accessible to increasing numbers of people. Second homes for weekend and holiday use have proliferated in these wooded uplands, bringing new features of social and economic life to villages that had experienced decades of depopulation. Reservoirs in the uplands form attractive focal areas for weekend residences and for water-based sports. Already upland areas within reasonable driving distance

of the towns and cities of industrial Wallonia and northern France are becoming parts of the 'dispersed city', as their agricultural settlements become transformed into commuter villages. Long-distance journey-to-work movements are well established in Belgium and will become even more important on both sides of the international boundary in the years to come, tying town and country together even more closely in a functional sense.

In the future it is to be hoped that more of a 'European' dimension may be introduced to the planning and management of this international problem region, occupying a key situation in north-western Europe that has been enhanced in the last ten years by the construction of the motorway network and will be strengthened even more in the future, when the Channel Tunnel is built and when further improvements in road and rail communications are made. For example, the Channel Tunnel and its approaches in northern France and Belgium will be of crucial importance for the high-speed (160 km per hour) inter-city rail network that has been proposed for the future.

The O.R.E.A.M.-Nord* plan has recognized important spatial differences within northern France and as a result has outlined different rates of likely population growth for the remainder of the twentieth century. It anticipated that the population of the coastal zone of the Nord will double between 1962 and A.D. 2000. During the same period the number of residents in the Nord as a whole will increase by about a half, and rates of growth in urban areas away from the coast will be roughly of that order, with rural areas losing population (Table 11). Broad objectives have been devised for planning each of the subregions in response to these estimates: important expansion of employment and housing in the coastal zone; renovation of the economy and the built environment in the central urban area; and rigorous conservation in the surrounding countryside for recreation and agricultural production. These proposals for the Nord region have not been made in ignorance of trends in operation in Belgium, yet plans have not been made to integrate the management of similar areas on both sides of the frontier. In similar fashion, planning schemes for neighbouring parts of Belgium have been conceived at a local or regional level without direct reference to conditions in France.

* Organisme d'Etudes d'Aménagement d'Aire Métropolitaine.

TABLE II

Estimated population changes in the Nord region,
A.D. 1962–2000 (millions)

	1962	2000
Nord region	3·6	5·6
Interior urban area	2·4	3·7
Coastal zone	0·55	1·1
Schelde valley	0·4	0·6
Rest of region	0·25	0·20

However, a case might be made for devising planning schemes that correspond to the economic sub-regions that can be seen to extend across the international boundaries of this problem region. These include: the textile axis from Ghent to Lille, extending into the ex-coalfield zone of the Pas-de-Calais; the coastal plain of the Nord; the mining and industrial areas of the Centre, Borinage, and neighbouring areas of France; and the eastern urbanized areas of Liège, Aachen, and Belgian and Dutch Limburg. Beyond these areas, the Antwerp–Brussels axis forms an area of important economic and demographic growth, and to the south the Ardennes upland represents a valuable open space for surrounding urban areas. Discussions certainly take place between French and Belgian planners on key issues of concern to areas on either side of the frontier, such as water supply, effluent disposal, and air pollution, but complete international co-operation for planning purposes is not envisaged in the immediate future. Schemes to establish a common policy for regional development applicable to all members of the European Economic Community will reduce to some extent the significance of the political frontier between France and Belgium, but the ancient boundary between Flemings and Walloons will remain as a stark cultural divide cutting through the Belgian section of this international problem region.

Further Work

The physical geography of the Franco-Belgian Border Region is examined in:

MONKHOUSE, F. J., *A Regional Geography of Western Europe*, (London, 3rd edit. 1968).

The historical background to the economy of the region is discussed in:

BLANCHARD, R., *La Flandre*, (Lille, 1906).

GILLET, M., 'The coal age and the rise of coal-fields in the North and the Pas-de-Calais', in F. Crouzet *et al.* (eds.), *Essays in European Economic History, 1789–1914*, (London, 1969).

POUNDS, N. J. G. and PARKER, W. N., *Coal and Steel in Western Europe*, (London 1957).

SMITH, C. T., *An Historical Geography of Western Europe before 1800*, (London, 1967).

WRIGLEY, E. A., *Industrial Growth and Population Change: a regional study of the coalfield areas on north-west Europe in the nineteenth century*, (Cambridge, 1961).

The modern economic and social conditions of northern France and Belgium are examined in:

GAY, F. and WAGRET, P. *Le Bénélux*, (Paris, 1970).

GENDARME, R., *La Région du Nord: essai d'analyse économique*, (Paris, 1954).

GEORGE, P., *France: a geographical study*, (London, 1973).

GEORGE, P. and SEVRIN, R., *Belgique, Pays-Bas, Luxembourg*, (Paris, 1967).

JUILLARD, E., *L'Europe rhénane*, (Paris, 1968).

LE LANNOU, M., *Les Régions Géographiques de la France*, (Paris, 1963), vol. I.

NISTRI, R. and PRECHEUR, C., *La Région du Nord/Nord-Est*, (Paris, 1965).

ORGANIZATION FOR ECONOMIC CO-OPERATION AND DEVELOPMENT, *Manpower Policy in Belgium*, (Paris, 1971).

SEVRIN, R., *Géographie de la Belgique et des Pays-Bas*, (Paris, 1969).

THOMPSON, I. B., *Modern France: a social and economic geography*, (London, 1970).

A detailed sociological study of employment and housing problems in the Nord is provided by:

MINCES, J., *Le Nord*, (Paris, 1967).

Articles by Professor Sporck (University of Liège) and Dr Mingret (University of Lyons) provide indispensable information on recent economic changes in Belgium:

MINGRET, P., 'Quelques problèmes de l'Europe: à travers l'exemple de Liège et de sa région', *Revue Géographique de Lyon*, **37**, (1962), pp. 5–74.

——'Les investissements américains en Belgique', *Revue Géographique de Lyon*, **45** (1970), pp. 243–278.

——'A factor in the regional evolution of Belgium: the geographical distribution of American industrial investments', *Terra* **84** (1972), pp. 14–22.

SPORCK, J. A., 'La reconversion économique des régions industrielles wallonnes', *L'Information Géographique*, **34** (1970), pp. 57–70.

Other references dealing with sections of the problem region include:

ANON., 'OREAM-Nord', *La Documentation Française*, **3635** (1969), pp. 1–72.

BRUYELLE, P., 'Lille-Roubaix-Tourcoing', *La Documentation Française*, **3206** (1965), pp. 1–80.

CHALINE, C., 'The Brussels Conurbation', *Geographical Journal*, **139** (1973), pp. 322–26.

CLOUT, H. D., 'Regional revival in the Nord region of France', *Norsk Geografisk Tidsskrift*, **25** (1971), pp. 145–158.

——'Nord coal miners prepare for 1983', *Geographical Magazine*, **44** (1972), pp. 398–406.

DICKINSON, R. E., 'The geography of commuting: the Netherlands and Belgium', *Geographical Review*, **47** (1957), pp. 521–538.

ELKINS, T. H., 'Liège and the problems of southern Belgium', *Geography*, **41** (1956), pp. 83–96.

——'National characteristics of industrial landscapes', in SPORCK, J. A. and MERENNE-SCHOUMAKER, B., (eds.) *Mélanges de Géographie offerts à M. Omer Tulippe*, Gembloux, (1967), vol. II, pp. 27–49.

FLEMING, D. K., 'Coastal steelworks in the Common Market countries', *Geographical Review*, **57** (1967), pp. 48–72.

LENTACKER, F., 'La frontière franco-belge', *L'Information Géographique*, **37** (1973), pp. 46–48.

MERENNE-SCHOUMAKER, B., 'L'évolution économique de la province de Liège depuis 1960', *Travaux Géographiques de Liège*, **159** (1972), pp. 215–234.

——'La région liégoise', *Travaux Géographiques de Liège*, 160 (1973), pp. 257–272.

MONIER, R., 'L'économie de la région du Nord et du Pas-de-Calais', *La Documentation Française*, **2837** (1961), pp. 1–59.

MUIR-WOOD, A. M. *et al.*, 'The Channel Tunnel', *Geographical Journal*, **139** (1973), pp. 258–279.

RILEY, R. C., 'Recent developments in the Belgian Borinage', *Geography*, **50** (1965), pp. 261–273.

——'Changes in the supply of coking coal in Belgium since 1945', *Economic Geography*, **43** (1967), pp. 261–270.

ROMUS, P., 'L'évolution économique régionale en Belgique depuis la création du Marché Commun', *Revue des Sciences Economiques*, **155** (1968), pp. 131–174.

SPORCK, J. A., 'L'organisation de l'espace dans la métropole liégoise', *Travaux Géographiques de Liège*, **159** (1972), pp. 355–383.

STEPHENSON, G. V., 'Cultural regionalism and the unitary state idea in Belgium', *Geographical Review*, **62** (1972), pp. 501–523.

THIERNESSE, L., 'La région économique boraine et ses problèmes', *Bulletin de la Société Géographique de Lille*, **3** (1960), pp. 54–86.

——'Problèmes de reconversion et d'aménagement de la région boraine', *Hommes et Terres du Nord*, **1** (1967), pp. 10–25.

THOMPSON, I. B., 'A geographical appraisal of recent trends in the coal basin of northern France', *Geography*, **50** (1965), pp. 252–260.

——'A review of problems of economic and urban development in the northern coalfield of France', *Southampton Research Series in Geography*, **1** (1965), pp. 31–60.

Hommes et Terres du Nord, published by the Geographical Society of Lille, the *Travaux Géographiques de Liège* and the *Bulletin de la Société Géographique de Liège* contain a wealth of detailed articles on northern France and Wallonia. Each article in these journals is abstracted in the appropriate series of *Geographical Abstracts*. Periodicals may be purchased from Geo Abstracts, University of East Anglia, Norwich NOR 88C.

The *Atlas du Nord de la France* (Editions Berger-Levrault, Paris, 1961) contains detailed maps of the region and a comprehensive text. The *Atlas de Belgique/Atlas van België* (Comité National de Géographie, Brussels) provides valuable cartographic material for Wallonia; and the *Grand Atlas de la France* (Sélection du Reader's Digest, Paris, 1973) includes a large number of maps showing social and economic conditions for northern France as well as other parts of the country. Large scale maps of the Franco-Belgian Border Region are published by the Institut Géographique National (Paris), the Institut Géographique Militaire (Brussels), and by Michelin.

Index